9. 95
5

D0107811

DATE DUE

7∤⊃		

GAYLORD   #3523PI   Printed in USA

MINDING GOD'S BUSINESS

RAY S. ANDERSON

WILLIAM B. EERDMANS PUBLISHING COMPANY
GRAND RAPIDS, MICHIGAN

Copyright © 1986 by Wm. B. Eerdmans Publishing Company
255 Jefferson Ave. S.E., Grand Rapids, Michigan 49503

All Scripture quotations are from the Revised Standard Version,
copyrighted 1946, 1952, © 1971, 1973 by the Division of Christian
Education, National Council of the Churches of Christ in the USA,
and used by permission.

Library of Congress Cataloging-in-Publication Data

Anderson, Ray Sherman.
  Minding God's business.

  Bibliography: p. 145
  Includes index.
  1. Church management.   2. Institution management.
3. Christian leadership.   I. Title.
BV652.A73   1986   267'.068   86-6367

ISBN 0-8028-0168-4

CONTENTS

v

PREFACE

If the title of this book seems pretentious, I can only trust that God will forgive. If it also seems pretentious that suggestions for managers of Christian organizations come from a teacher of theology, one wonders if forgiveness is enough!

What qualifications I have for thinking like a manager were not earned in managing a Christian organization, nor in seminary, but in managing a modest farming operation for seven years following college. Some of my friends from those days feel that if working in a "nonprofit" business qualifies one for a discussion of managing Christian organizations, I have a decided advantage! I have, however, met a payroll, if that is of any help. But I also tend to value my education in common-sense principles of business more than my acquaintance with balancing dollars and cents on a bottom line.

For what it is worth, I must confess to being more of a theologian than a manager. Yet I have never been able to shake loose from a certain curiosity about how things work and why they cannot be made to work better. Perhaps it was this curiosity, if not a natural affinity, for the business side of creation that enticed me to join in a venture at Fuller Theological Seminary that linked theology to management.

The genesis of this book lies in the beginning of the Institute for Christian Organizational Development at Fuller, and my participation as a teacher in one of its seminars. I openly acknowledge that I brought nothing to that first seminar except a depth of commitment to the biblical teaching that God has created this world for a purpose and that we have been given the mandate to work out his purpose. Through the interaction and stimulation of those leaders and managers of Christian organizations who participated in that first seminar, I began to prepare my response. It could not have been done otherwise.

While the material in this book has been prepared primarily

for those who are in management and leadership positions in Christian organizations, what is said here may very well apply to pastors of local churches as well. Although Christian organizations have unique characteristics as distinguished from local churches, the basic principles of Christian management and leadership can equally be applied to the task of managing the church.

This book deals primarily with the *what* of managing Christian organizations rather than with the *how* of managing. It should not be read as a book on basic management principles. There are a multitude of such resources available. Nor should this book be read as a "hands-on" manual for the task of management. What I have provided here is a theological and biblical basis for understanding the unique characteristics of Christian organizations, as well as a discussion of what it means to manage such organizations in a *Christian* way.

I wish here to express my appreciation to those who have contributed to my own thought through their encouragement and challenge in our seminar sessions. Particularly, I owe a debt of gratitude to my teaching colleague, Ed Dayton, Vice President of Mission and Evangelism, World Vision International. He has been a gracious and kind mentor in assisting me to shape my theological thoughts to fit more appropriately in a management context. It is to Dr. Walter Wright, however, that I must pay final tribute. As director of the Institute for Christian Organizational Development, he first encouraged me to continue with my attempt to work out a theology for Christian organizational development. It was his vision for a book in this area that challenged me to continue beyond my first efforts. Both of these men have contributed to this work through their accurate and insightful comments. I am still responsible, of course, for its shortcomings and limitations.

This book is dedicated to those who bear the often agonizing but always thrilling task of "minding God's business." May it be a good business.

Ray S. Anderson

MINDING GOD'S BUSINESS

CHAPTER ONE

WHAT IN THE WORLD IS GOD DOING?

On a Sunday afternoon, after feasting on several helpings of fried chicken, the pastor walked with the farmer out to view the crops. Standing on the top of a small rise in the land, they could look over the panorama of green pastures dotted with grazing cattle, meticulously cultivated row crops that pushed the horizon back against the blue sky, and a charming apple orchard blossoming with promise of the ripe fruit to come.

After several minutes of silence, the man of the cloth exclaimed, "What wonders God can do with his creation, and how beautiful are his works!"

"I don't doubt that is so," replied the farmer, "but you should have seen this when he had it to himself."

Those of us who have responsibility for leadership and management of Christian organizations often feel the same way. It is quite appropriate to give God the credit as well as the glory, but under our breath we have been heard to whisper, "If God is the head of this organization then why am I doing all of the work?"

What in the world is God doing?

Has he created the world and left it up to us to manage it? Perhaps. One could argue that case from the creation story in Genesis. "God finished his work," we are told, "and he rested . . . from all his work" (Gen. 2:2-3). What is more, if there is further work to be done—and there is—it is to be done by the human persons placed within the creation for this specific task. To the first couple, God said, "Be fruitful and multiply, and fill the earth and subdue it" (Gen. 1:28).

So running and managing this created world is our business, after all—right? Well, not quite.

"My Father is working still, and I am working," said Jesus

1

(John 5:17). Aha! There it is. God *is* working, not resting. So, perhaps it is his business, after all, to see that the work is done effectively, if not also efficiently.

This is what this book is all about—minding God's business. We will need to explore what the nature of God's business is and what "minding" it entails. We will focus on the nature and role of Christian organizations as those that "mind God's business" in a specialized way. We will define these organizations with respect to God's own work of creation and redemption as well as with respect to the church as God's mission in the world.

In this chapter, our purpose is to show that God's work is centered in the person and work of Jesus Christ as the one who brings the good news, or gospel. The gospel is that God has entered into history in order to accomplish the restoration and reconciliation of his created world, including human society, to the end that God is glorified and lost humanity becomes a "people of God." This gospel, which has been completed in the person and work of Jesus Christ, is taken up by those commissioned to be his apostles by the resurrected Christ, as the power of God for salvation (Rom. 1:16). Through the ministry of these apostles, in the power of the Holy Spirit received at Pentecost, the church is born as the agent of the gospel and as a sign of the kingdom of God in the world. God's kingdom is his sovereign rule over and within the world, which was manifest in Israel and present in the fullness of power in Jesus Christ (Matt. 12:28). Jesus proclaimed the "gospel of the kingdom" through his own ministry of teaching and healing (Matt. 4:23).

The thesis of this chapter is that Christian organizations exist to carry out the continuing apostolic task of the "gospel of the kingdom" as part of the church of Jesus Christ. To develop this thesis we will need, first of all, to consider the question of how the church relates to the apostolic mandate of proclaiming the gospel of the kingdom, on the one hand, and to the work of the kingdom as mission in the world, on the other hand. Then we will seek to define the nature of Christian organizations and their role within this apostolic mandate. This will prepare us for the following chapter, in which we will do some theological reflection on the nature and purpose of Christian organizations.

God has finished his work, we are told, both in his act of creating and in his act of redemption upon the cross. The gospel of the kingdom is a "finished gospel," so to speak. The work for our salvation and for the reconciliation of the world to God is God's work—and he has completed it. Yet, we might say that Christ saw his own work as "minding God's business." And the apostle Paul taught that Christ has given gifts to the church "for the work of ministry" (Eph. 4:12).

How, then, are we to understand this? If God has finished with his work, and yet is still working, does his work depend upon our work, or does our work depend upon his? Does he do the planning and managing and we do the work, or do we do the planning and managing and God do the work? Let me put the question another way. If I say that my work is "Christian" work, or that my business is a "Christian" business, does this mean that God is the chief executive officer and that I am his administrative assistant? Does the adjective "Christian" give to any organization or business an added dimension of management skills because one can then assume that it is now "God's business"?

Wait a minute! One thing at a time! There are several issues here that we need to look at more closely.

First, we must look at what it means to say that God has finished his work and has entered into his rest. The "rest" into which God entered when he finished his creation surely cannot mean that God has discontinued his interest or his activity in the world. In fact, Jesus made it quite clear that God, his Father, continues to work in the world. Nor did Jesus cease from his own activity on the assumption that it was, if you please, God's business. The Sabbath rest into which God entered when creation was finished was not a state of inactivity or complete passivity, but, rather, the work by which he brings to realization his purpose in creation through the formation of his people.

For example, when a woman conceives a child and enters into the creative period of gestation, she still faces the labor of actually bringing forth the child into a living world of its own possibility. When the baby is born, she has "finished," so to speak, with her labor of creation and can enter into her "rest." But this is not a period of inactivity! Now the process of formation begins—and continues. And so, from the perspective of the child, "my mother is working still," even though she has, in a sense, finished with the labor of creation.

This concept of formation is a concept of work that moves toward that which is "finished"—that is, toward that which is both the original and the final determination of character and nature. A child's humanity is settled at birth, but not its character, which is under the determination of love and intentionality that "knows the end from the beginning." We know what good character is before the process of formation begins. This is because the ultimate purpose and destiny for the process of life has been disclosed as God's purpose and determination for us. The process by which purpose is formed into character is the "work" of parenting. But God also participates in this creative and formative process. Thus, parenting itself is the "work of God," even though it is at the same time the work and responsibility of the parents. By attaching the adjective "Christian" to the work of parenting, however, one has not surrendered to God the responsibility for the work, nor has one suddenly acquired a new and totally different set of rules for this work. Rather, Christians should understand the work of parenting to be a process of formation that simultaneously is God's work.

How does this analogy relate to "God's business in the world"? Look at it this way. God "gave birth" to the church at Pentecost. The conception of this "child" occurred as he entered into his rest at the time of creation, and developed through the process of calling forth a people to bear his name (Israel) and of establishing a realm over which he would reign (the kingdom). Through the labor pains of the birth, life, death, and resurrection of Jesus, his work also is "finished" (John 19:30). Yet the work of God in the world continues with the sending of the Spirit at Pentecost and the process of the formation of the kingdom of God as the end (*eschaton*) of all things.

In this way one can see the church as the process of formation by which God's purpose becomes actualized in and through the world. Jesus can cry out from the cross, "It is finished," and yet he continues to work through the presence and power of the Holy Spirit in the life and work of Christians in the world.

In this sense we can say that Christ is the essential link that connects the work of creation to the work of God's final consummation of all things. In the same way, Christ is the essential link connecting human society, with all of its structures and agencies, to God's ultimate purpose of forming a people to share his own eternal glory. By "essential link" I mean to say that in Jesus Christ we see the one by whom all things were created and the one to whom all creation points as the Lord (Col. 1:15-20).

A schematic representation of this point looks something like this:

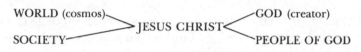

WORLD (cosmos)   GOD (creator)

JESUS CHRIST

SOCIETY   PEOPLE OF GOD

Figure 1

When we see that Jesus Christ is the center of all reality, as the above diagram shows, then we see why the adjective *Christian* should not be used to qualify a noun (e.g., "Christian organization") without a clear understanding of what the substantive reality is that stands behind the adjective. The noun that the adjective *Christian* modifies cannot of itself give content to the word *Christian*. This is because the person of Christ himself is the substantive reality of the word *Christian*. In the same way, one should not use the word *Christian* to represent principles or values that merely describe a function, such as the management of an organization. This is not to say that the function of management ought not to be done in a Christian way, or that an organization that seeks to be an agent of Christ's mission in the world ought not to be called a Christian organization.

At best, what is meant by "Christian organization" is that the organization is in some way part of the process of God's work. This work, through Jesus Christ, is the work by which he continues to bring into actualization his purpose—which was "finished" in the work of Christ through his death and resurrection, and yet continues through the process of the church's ministry in the world. Thus, when we use the adjective *Christian* we must always have in view the concept of Christ himself as the essential link and the substantive reality upon which the term rests and from which it derives its meaning. This is the purpose of Figure 1 above.

At this point we need to examine more fully what is meant by the word *church,* and to explain how the church relates to God's work in the world. I have alluded to the way in which the church came into existence through the power of the gospel as carried out in the mission of the apostles. The church participates in this apostolic mandate through the following three-fold sequence:

$$\text{GOSPEL} \longrightarrow \text{CHURCH} \longrightarrow \text{MISSION}$$

Let us begin on the left with the gospel. For the apostle Paul, the "gospel" is that reality of God which was revealed to him and by which he was commissioned to minister to the Gentiles (see Gal. 1:11-12, 15-16). This "gospel" is the substance of the work of God in Christ by which he died for sinners and was raised up by the power of God for our salvation (1 Cor. 15:1-3).

In our diagram the gospel is the source of the apostolic mandate to proclaim Christ to the world through specific mission activities. That is, the direction is from gospel toward mission, with the church, as the body of Christ, the connecting link. The mission of the church is thus grounded in the gospel as its source and authority. In the diagram, the church is strategically placed between gospel and mission. The apostolic mandate is actually the gospel mandate by which the church comes into existence and through which it extends its own life into the work of mission. The church is not the end result of the gospel by virtue of its own existence; it exists so that the gospel can be carried out in mission to the world. The church is an agent of the work of the gospel, not the final form of the gospel itself as an organization or an institution. Nor is mission capable of sustaining itself as an activity or organization except as it is grounded in the life of the church through the power and authority of the gospel.

The church, then, comes into being as the power of the gospel is born as the mission of the Holy Spirit (Pentecost). The apostolic character of the church is its role in the process of gospel taking formation through mission. The role of the original apostles in this process is unique and foundational for the church. However, the church itself is apostolic in its life and purpose as it continues to give expression to the gospel as Christ's own mission in the world. If the church should lose its orientation to the gospel as the reality of Christ's finished work of redemption, it would lose its apostolic character. Likewise, if the church should turn in on its own existence and fail to extend its life and purpose into mission in the world, it would no longer be an apostolic church. This is what we mean when we say that the apostolic mandate is grounded in the gospel but is directed toward mission in the world as the work of Christ.

However, remember our point that the adjective *Christian* must be related back to Christ himself, who is the substantial reality of the word. In the same way, a work of mission is not a "Christian mission" or a "Christian organization" except that it exists as the power of the gospel and as a form of the church in fulfilling the apostolic mandate.

Thus, in addition to the apostolic mandate, by which gospel is directed toward mission, there is a theological mandate, which is directed from mission toward gospel. It requires us to reflect back upon the gospel as the authority, content, and power of the mission. We will use the same diagram but take as our beginning point mission rather than gospel:

GOSPEL ⟵—— CHURCH ⟵—— MISSION

From the perspective of mission, which is the work of Christ in the world in fulfillment of the apostolic mandate, we now are directed back through the church to the gospel. Those who are involved in mission as the work of Christ must reflect back upon the relation of that mission activity to the church and to the gospel, which is the power and authority for the mission of the church. This "theological reflection" is the task of the church as it carries out the mission of Christ in the world; that is, the church is to ground that mission in the authority of the gospel. To do so requires biblical study, prayer, and a critical examination of the mission activity in light of biblical teachings and principles. This is because Scripture, the written Word of God, is a result of the apostolic witness to the gospel, through the inspiration of the Holy Spirit. The Bible is the authoritative and normative canon for the content of the gospel even as the Spirit of Christ in the church is the authoritative and enabling power for the exercise of mission.

The movement of theological reflection takes place continuously along with the apostolic mandate. Both activities are essential to the formation of gospel as mission, and together they serve as a self-correcting process. For example, Jesus performed the work of God, his Father, through his ministry of teaching, healing, and feeding the hungry. "My Father is working, and I am working," is the way he put it. But when he healed a man on the Sabbath and was charged with breaking the law of God, Jesus responded by reflecting theologically on his mission, saying, "The sabbath was made for man, not man for the sabbath" (Mark 2:27). Here Jesus argues—theologically—that God's rest is a process by which human persons become whole and related to God. This process is itself a "work of God."

Thus, the value of theological reflection is that it grounds mission in the liberating power of gospel, and keeps it from becoming rigid and self-justifying, embedded in the rituals of institutional self-preservation. When mission becomes merely an extension of the church's own need for self-preservation, it loses both its apostolic character as well as its power as a sign of the presence and power of the kingdom of God.

We can picture the dynamic relation of the apostolic and theological mandate in this way:

Figure 2

This schematic places the church in a strategic location between the gospel and mission—a very important concept. The church is neither the origin nor the source of mission—it must be anchored in its own source, which is the gospel. But, on the other hand, the church is not the institutional form of gospel—it must be anchored in the work of mission.

The mission of God in the world, broadly defined, is his finished work of redemption through Jesus Christ, which is proclaimed as the gospel. Through Christ's gift of his Spirit, this work, which has been completed, continues to accomplish its purpose through the transformation of sinful persons into a new community of social and spiritual health: the church, the body of Christ (Eph. 1:15–2:10). This work of mission must always be critically assessed in terms of its relation to the church as the body of Christ and to the gospel as the power of Christ unto salvation (Rom. 1:16-17). The work of mission cannot make an "end run," as it were, and bypass the church as the body of Christ. Nor should one suppose that the apostolic mandate itself could take the form of a mission without being accountable to the body of Christ in the process of the formation of the gospel.

No one had as clear a grasp of the gospel and of the apostolic mandate as did the apostle Paul. He saw clearly what we now have as the testimony of the four Gospels in the New Testament, that the life, death, and resurrection of Jesus is the gospel of the kingdom of God. And no one had as compelling a call to the work of mission as did this same apostle, who wrote, "Woe to me if I do not preach the gospel!" (1 Cor. 9:16). As the Apostle to the Gentiles, Paul saw his mission as a calling to preach the gospel, yet "not where Christ has already been named, lest I build on another man's foundation" (Rom. 15:20). But these words are found at the end of a letter to the church at Rome, a church he had not founded, but that he expected to assist him in his projected mission to Spain (Rom. 15:24).

In his letter to the church in Rome, Paul demonstrates the differential between the apostolic and the theological mandates. In obedience to the apostolic mandate, he does not create a mission and an organization to fulfill it that "leapfrogs" over the church, but rather sees his own mission as part of the process of the formation of the body of Christ. In this sense he seeks to work with and through the church. But here, too, we see the theological mandate at work, for his letter is far more than a pragmatic appeal for the spiritual and material means to carry out his mission. As a result, it becomes a highly theological document, reflecting back on the power of the gospel and thinking out again its implications in terms of the earliest gospel tradition, which lay behind the formation of the church itself.

The point is this. The church is the crucial center in the differential between the apostolic and the theological mandates. It is, however, but one of many Christian organizations, broadly speaking; and these other organizations must also be under the same mandates. The nature of a Christian organization that seeks to carry out the mission of Christ in the world can be described only in terms of both apostolic and theological mandates. Thus, we need to delineate more clearly what we mean by *church* and *Christian organization*.

For the purposes of this discussion, we will define *church* as the form that the body of Christ takes in the world under the authority of and with the power of Christ, through Word (Scripture) and Spirit. We do not mean by this simple definition to disdain ecclesiastical distinctions that exist between "churches." Our purpose is to preserve for the word *church* the "middle ground," so to speak, between gospel and mission, as set forth above. In this way, we have attempted to make it clear that the church, as the body of Christ, is always subject to the critical assessment of whether it is faithful to the gospel, and whether it is effective in mission.

We can here make a further point in delineating the concept of *church*. Because the church, as the body of Christ, is always a specific formation of people through the effective power of the gospel rather than merely an idea or a concept, it always has a geographical center. It exists on earth, not in the air. And it exists somewhere before it does everywhere. Recognition of this geographical location as well as its demographic composition led to the concept of the church being a parish, with a parochial identity. Paul wrote not just to the Christians in Rome, but to the "gathered Christians"—that is, the church—in Rome. Moreover, he assured them that "all the churches of Christ" greeted them (Rom. 16:16); further, he gave them personal greetings from Gaius, as a host "to the whole church" (Rom. 16:23). The parochial form of the church, then, is a specific gathering of Christians in a localized setting.

In addition, there is also what we might call a nonparochial form of the church, what Paul called "the whole church." To illustrate this, think of Paul's activities as an organizer of a specific ministry of relief for the impoverished Christians at Jerusalem. No single person or church is responsible for raising the needed funds. While Paul takes some responsibility upon himself (in his letter to the church at Rome he writes that he had taken personal responsibility to raise contributions among the churches of Macedonia and Achaia; Rom. 15:25-27), he makes it clear in his second letter to the Corinthian church that Titus is his partner in this endeavor. In this same letter he also mentions other "messengers" of the churches who are assisting (2 Cor. 8:23), and refers to the "brother who is famous among all the churches for his preaching of the gospel," who has been "appointed by the churches" to travel with them (2 Cor. 8:18). Not only that; in his first letter to the same church, Paul says that he will send those whom the church in Corinth selected from among their own fellowship to accompany the gift to Jerusalem (1 Cor. 16:3).

What, then, do we make of this? Certainly a good deal of activity and not a little organization has gone into this effort. It has all the earmarks of being apostolic, of being an activity demanded by the gospel of Christ. It also has the marks of the theological mandate, as shown by Paul's extended theological argument in 2 Corinthians 8–9, where he appeals in the name of Christ himself, who "though he was rich, yet for your sake he became poor" (8:9).

Yet no "church" in the parochial sense took the responsibility to organize and carry out this mission. Clearly, this is an example of what we mean by a nonparochial form of the church carrying out both apostolic and theological mandates. In this sense, it occupies the "middle ground" in our schematic model shown in Figure 2 above. Quite clearly there is some degree of tension between the parochial and the nonparochial forms of the church, as is evident from Paul's sensitivity to the parochial churches. Yet he does not hesitate to undertake the activity as a legitimate expression of the "total church," creating a new organization to carry it out.

At this point an important comment should be made concerning the use of the term *parachurch*. I am suggesting here that we no longer use this term, for reasons that are as surely theological as they are practical. The term *parachurch* implies at best that which is alongside the church, and at worst that which is not the church. This concept violates the theological mandate as well as the apostolic mandate as we have developed the paradigm above. Furthermore, the concept of *parachurch* tends to move in the direction of autonomous and independent organizations that link gospel directly with mission with no place for the church at all. Or, as has happened in some cases, the mission becomes the parochial form of the church, but without the biblical marks of the church, and thus with no doctrine of the church.

Therefore, rather than speak of organizations that have their center and activity beyond or between the parochial form of the church as "parachurch" organizations, should we not speak of such organizations as *nonparochial* forms of the apostolic church in mission?

Yes, I hear the protests! The terminology is unwieldly and the concept is archaic. What is a parish in our society of mobility and multimedia communication? Besides, everyone knows what a parachurch ministry is; who will know what we are talking about when we speak of World Vision International as a nonparochial organization?

Good point. The term *nonparochial organization* says absolutely nothing by itself. In fact, it tends to instill a negative concept in the hearer's mind. It still sounds like "nonchurch" to the one who finally figures out that *parochial* has something to do with the church. For this reason, then, I prefer the prefix *para* to that of *non*parochial.

The Greek pronoun *para,* which when attached to the word *church* created a concept of a new entity that is not the church, is a rich and suggestive word. When joined to the Greek word for being, *ousia,* it becomes *parousia.* Thus, we look forward to the appearing or manifestation (*parousia*) of Christ. Paul uses this word in his exhortation tote curch at Thessalonica with respect to the "coming of our Lord Jesus Christ" (1 Thess. 4:15; 2 Thess. 2:1). Thus, *para* can have the sense of the presence or manifestation of something.

The church in its parochial form will always be limited and bound to its geographic and demographic center, which is the church in its sense of being a "gathered" body of Christians. In this sense, the church as parish has stability and tends to be what we might call "community-specific" in its nature. By this

we mean to suggest that the local church as a gathered congregation has, among its other functions, the unique function
of creating and upbuilding a community of people as the body
of Christ. Thus, the parochial form of the church is community-specific in a sense that the paraparochial form of the church
is not. This holds true despite the fact that a Christian organization as a paraparochial form of the church also experiences
a community of Christian life and fellowship. However, that is
not its specific function.

The paraparochial form of the church, on the other hand,
might be termed "mission-specific." A Christian organization,
for example, ordinarily has a specific mission as its unique
purpose. By designating Christian organizations as mission-
specific, and by calling them paraparochial forms of the
church, we have avoided two problems. First, we have avoided
the negative implications of calling such activity *nonparochial*.
Second, we have avoided the unfortunate implications of saying *parachurch*, as though such mission-specific organizations
are not really the church. *Paraparochial* retains the rich and
powerful biblical concept of presence and manifestation
through the use of the prefix *para*. So, for better or worse,
paraparochial it shall be.

Paul's mission-specific activity, organized as a project to
raise gifts from churches in Macedonia and Achaia for the
relief of the poor in the church at Jerusalem, was thus a paraparochial expression of the "total church." As such, it was an
organization that existed in its own right and developed administrative and management functions of its own appropriate to its task. However, because it was paraparochial rather
than nonparochial, it developed close links with local churches
and sought to bring the gifts and resources of these churches
to bear in the ministry of the total church. We could assume
that whatever organizational form the mission outreach into
Spain would have taken had Paul been able to carry out that
vision, it would also have taken the form of a paraparochial
organization.

It would be good at this point to refocus our discussion on
the primary purpose for this chapter and to restate our basic
thesis. We set forth the purpose of showing how the work of
God is centered on the person and work of Jesus Christ as one

who brings into fulfillment the gospel of the kingdom. We have elaborated on this purpose by demonstrating that Christ is the essential link between God as Creator and the created world. We also have shown how Christ is the essential link between God's purpose of redemption and the accomplished work of reconciliation through his death and resurrection. Through this work of Christ, the church came into existence as the continuing agent of reconciliation. As a result, we can say that the work of redemption, even as with the work of creation, is "finished." Yet we can also understand that God continues to work toward the fulfillment of his own purpose through the historical presence and activity of the church as a sign of the kingdom of God. The gospel of redemption is God's business, and the church in both its parochial and para-parochial forms "minds God's business" as it extends its life and purpose into the mission of God in the world.

The basic thesis of this chapter has been the assertion that Christian organizations, as a paraparochial form of the church, exist to carry out the continuing apostolic task of the "gospel of the kingdom." We developed this thesis by showing how the church relates, on the one hand, to the apostolic mandate of proclaiming the gospel, and, on the other hand, to the work of the kingdom of God as mission. We then defined Christian organizations as the paraparochial form of the church that centers on specific mission activity in the world, rather than upon the function of building community. (Though we hasten to add once more that the mission-specific activity of Christian organizations does not exclude the function of Christian community as part of the organization's life and purpose.)

Thus, Christian organizations exist to carry out the apostolic mandate of the gospel within the broader context of the church. We have sought to provide a rationale for the existence of Christian organizations as a legitimate order of ministry within the apostolic mandate by which the church understands its nature and mission within the world. This rationale will become the foundation for developing a theology of Christian organizations, including a theology of the management of Christian organizations.

In concluding our discussion in this chapter, let's review and expound on the key concepts that have developed out of our reflection on the nature of Christian organizations. This will prepare the way for the next chapter, a reflection on the theological mandate for Christian organizations.

1. Through Jesus Christ, God has completed his work of redemption. This brought forth the gospel as the apostolic mandate by which the continuing work of God in Christ seeks to fulfill God's purpose as a mission of redemption and reconciliation in the world. The church emerges out of this apostolic mandate as the body of Christ, consisting of those who have been transformed by the power of the gospel and brought into a new experience of community in Christ. At the same time, the church exists for the purpose of extending its own life into the mission of God in the world.

2. The church, in this broad context, is always ambiguous and provisional with regard to its form and structure. Yet it is always unambiguously related to the power of the gospel as its source and the mission of Christ in the world as its *raison d'être*. That is, there will be many kinds of churches—national, local, denominational—but only one head, Jesus Christ. There will be many kinds of organizational structures and strategies, but only one task—to complete the work of Christ in proclaiming and practicing the gospel of salvation, reconciliation, and restoration of the world to God.

3. Both parochial and paraparochial forms of the church will occur in the sector that relates the church to mission. In the sector that relates the church to gospel, parochial and paraparochial distinctions tend to disappear. To identify these sectors more clearly we need to refer back to Figure 2 (p. 8). When we follow the apostolic mandate from gospel to mission, the sector between church and mission is the one in which the distinction is more sharply defined. For example, in the biblical example we referred to above, when Paul organizes the contribution for the saints in Jerusalem, this activity takes place in the sector between church and mission. However, when he writes to the church at Rome with a view to their cooperation in a prospective mission to Spain, he reflects back on the gospel in such a way that what he says applies equally to the parochial as well as to the paraparochial form of the church. This is very instructive for us, for it shows that there can be a great diversity in the strategies by which the mission is

carried out without the need to achieve organizational unity at
the level of mission. For the unity between parochial and paraparochial forms of the mission is to be found in the gospel,
which is the common source of authority and power.

4. A parochial form of the church will have a form and
purpose that ordinarily includes a mission in the world as well
as a concern for the formation of the people of God into a
community of worship, edification, discipling, and equipping
of the body of Christ. However, the form of the church in its
parochial task serves as a limitation upon its mission. Like the
church at Antioch, it can "send out" but it cannot "go out"
(Acts 13:1-3). When Paul and Barnabas are sent out, a paraparochial organization is created that has an interesting relation to the church at Antioch. Paul and Barnabas report back
to this church, yet neither the new churches formed nor the
mission organization itself appears to become part of the organization of the church at Antioch. If the paraparochial organization becomes itself a parochial organization (as happened in
Ephesus and Corinth, for example), then the task of edification, discipling, and equipping of the body becomes a primary
task.

5. A Christian organization, as we will use the term from this
point on, refers primarily to the paraparochial (often called
parachurch) forms of the church's apostolic mandate to carry
out the mission of Christ in the world. This definition includes
denominational agencies such as the Christian Reformed
World Relief Committee. But it also includes organizations
that have no direct denominational connection, such as World
Vision International, Youth For Christ International, and
Young Life.

6. A Christian organization in this sense can be said to be a
gathering of Christian persons in common cause, who have a
distinctively Christian identity and mission. The social structure of this community is organized and directed in such a way
that the mission of the community is transformed from subjective intentions to objective operations in which intended results are produced, capable of assessment and verification.
Paul had a subjective intention and purpose with regard to
meeting the needs of the poor in Jerusalem. But his vision was
not yet a Christian organization. When this intention was
transformed into objective operations through the network of

assigned and delegated tasks, a Christian organization came into existence.

7. The function of directing such an organization is what we mean by "management." What makes Christian organizations distinctive is the content of the common cause. We designated this as the unique nature of a Christian organization as being mission-specific. This distinctive also includes the effectual modes and strategies of operation—the gifts and power of the Holy Spirit—as well as the ultimate (eschatological) reality of the product or service that results (the kingdom of God).

8. Development of Christian organizations, therefore, is essentially the development of a community of Christian people whose organizational goal is mission-intensive. Organization in the Christian organization is the servant of the mission, which is the creative power behind the organization.

9. Christian organizations share not only the apostolic mandate of the church but also the responsibility for the theological mandate of interpreting the task of mission on the basis of the gospel. It is noteworthy that the primary documents in the New Testament in which theological reflection upon the gospel takes place are created out of the mission of the church (e.g., Romans and Galatians). If paraparochial organizations are considered as the form of the church in mission, then the responsibility—if not also the competence—for doing this on-going theological reflection lies with the paraparochial sector. The theological training centers of the church (colleges and seminaries) are then also paraparochial institutions and should have a working link with the other paraparochial organizations sharing a partnership in theological reflection.

10. Christian organizations often are structured more along the lines of "entrepreneurial management" rather than "ecclesiastical management." By "entrepreneurial" I mean leadership that is primarily vested in an enterprising type of person who demonstrates strength in creating new ideas or programs and who can motivate others to develop and manage them. Ecclesiastical management is a form and style of leadership that is developed out of a biblical or theological understanding of church order and policy. To the extent that managers of Christian organizations tend to be of the entrepreneurial type, they should have a clear understanding of

both apostolic and theological mandates by which they can
effectively accomplish their ministry of management. Managers of Christian organizations do not need to be theologians in
the professional sense, but they need to be as competent in the
task of theological reflection as they are in management theory and practice.

Yes, we are minding God's business—or we ought to be! But
what is the "business" with which God is busy as he prepares
the way for the people he has loved in Jesus Christ to enter into
his rest? We should now do some theological reflection on the
nature and purpose of Christian organizations. And as God
said to Job, "Gird up your loins like a man, I will question you,
and you shall declare to me" (38:3).

But don't panic—a little theology never hurt anyone!

CHAPTER TWO

A LITTLE THEOLOGY
NEVER HURT ANYONE!

The ordinary Christian fears theology for several reasons. But foremost of all is the fear that it is some kind of spiritual disease that is caught at a theological seminary for which, like the common cold, there is no ready cure. There is even more to fear from a professor of theology, some would say, for in this case the disease has become a professional occupation with a degree behind it! I have no doubt but that these fears are justified. We who are doctors of theology too often attempt to "scrut" the inscrutable. Confusing ponderous prose for prophetic perspicuity (oh no, I did it again!), we tantalize and torment our hearers with sophistication masked as erudition.

It's time for some "plain-speak" about theology.

God is his own self-interpreter; no one has ever seen him, but "the only Son, who is in the bosom of the Father, he has made him known" (John 1:18). This "only Son," of course, is Jesus of Nazareth, who once said, "no one knows the Son except the Father, and no one knows the Father except the Son and any one to whom the Son chooses to reveal him" (Matt. 11:27). Jesus is the Word *(Logos)* that was with God in the beginning, the Word *(Logos)* that became flesh and dwelt among us (John 1:1, 14). Since the Greek word for God is *theos*, Jesus is the *"logos of theos"*; he is the interpreter of God as the Word of God that became flesh and continues to disclose the nature and purpose of God to us.

In the simplist sense, theology *(theo-logos)* is the science of the knowledge of God that takes place through our reflection upon the gospel of Jesus Christ from the perspective of our participation in the saving work of God. (All right, so it's not simple! Let me put it another way.) Theology is the task of being responsible to act and think in accordance with the way in which God *(theos)* thinks and acts.

Theology, therefore, is the task and responsibility of every Christian, for the experience of God through faith in Jesus Christ brings all human experience under the crucial question: Is it in accordance with the revealed nature and purpose of God? This is what we mean when we say that theology is a "science" of the knowledge of God. It is, in fact, the critical science of bringing our experience and our human perspective under the critical examination of the divine *Logos.*

Theology is not our interpretation of the acts of God—for we cannot of ourselves bring God under examination. He is not at our disposal, so to speak, in such a way that we can interpret him. Rather, God is his own self-interpreter through his own *Logos,* which has become incarnate in Jesus Christ. Therefore, theology is the task and responsibility of bringing our minds as well as our actions under the direction of the divine *Logos.* This is a personal and devotional act, of course, but it is also an act and process of critical thinking.

In doing this type of thinking, we must exercise care that we do not extend our own thoughts and presuppositions into the content of God's act and thoughts. And we must be careful not to obscure that which has become plain and clear through God's revelation in Christ. But we must also exercise courage, for we are summoned by God to think his thoughts after him, and to remember that the act of God as his ministry of love and reconciliation toward the world is a continuing act demanding a continuing act of thought on our part. Thus, theology always has in view the act of God in Christ that has been given to us through the inspired and infallible Scripture. But theology always is a contemporary process of locating the present act (ministry) of God in the world and thinking out the connections between this ministry and the larger context of God's ministry of reconciliation.

In the first chapter we suggested that there is an apostolic mandate by which the gospel of Christ takes formation in the world through mission, with the church as the agent of this process. We also suggested that there is a theological mandate that works back from mission, through church, to the gospel. The primary task of this theological reflection on gospel, we

said, arises out of the mission; we referred to the apostle Paul
and to his letter to the Roman church as an example of this.

Our purpose in this chapter is to do some theological reflection of our own, from the perspective of the nature and function of Christian organizations as one form (paraparochial) of
the mission of the church in the world. Specifically, we will
attempt to do three things: first, to show how Christian organizations are part of the church as God's covenant people; second, to show how the management of Christian organizations
relates to the purpose of God; and third, to describe the leadership function of managing Christian organizations in terms
of God's will.

Through this discussion we will help managers of Christian
organizations answer several questions:

1. How does a Christian organization of a paraparochial
nature relate to the kingdom of God and to the church?

2. In what ways can Christian organizations use the so-called
secular aspects of managing without compromising the integrity of the Christian organization?

3. Do Christian organizations have access to Christian forms
of management and leadership—that is, are there "Christian
management principles"?

4. Is it really "spiritual" to use management practices that
are also used in non-Christian organizations?

5. How are the values and goals for Christian organizational
management determined when an organization has to be
"successful" to survive but also is called to "die with Christ" to
the world?

In order to bring some clarity and logical order to our discussion, we will consider four theses relating to a theology of
Christian organizational development. Each thesis will be
stated formally, followed by an elaboration of its implications.
I hope that this will provide a model for theological reflection
and a foundation for subsequent development of a theology of
management for Christian organizations.

Thesis 1. The existing cosmos is a world order originally designed by God as Creator and Lord; this order is determin-

ative for the existence of human persons (social order) as well as of the world order.

Here we recall Figure 1 from the first chapter:

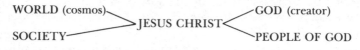

Figure 1

Human society is a social order that is linked with the world order (the cosmos). The same creative Word (Jesus Christ) by whom God brought the cosmos into being also established human society. Just as the world as cosmos has its antecedent in God as Creator, so the human social order has its antecedent in God's purpose to create a people for himself. Jesus Christ is the "essential link" in this structure of reality.

While the created order, including the social order, is given its own reality by God's creative Word, it also exists under the creative tension of realizing in its own present worldly existence ultimate values, purposes, and ethical responsibilities that are rooted in God's own eternal Word. As Jesus said, "Heaven and earth will pass away, but my words will not pass away" (Mark 13:31).

Human society, as part of this cosmos, does not contain within itself absolute principles and forms by which it can determine its own destiny. Rather, its principles and forms are provisional and temporal in light of the eternal reality—the *eschaton* of God as the final "end" or consummation of all things. From this perspective, we say that human society with all of its forms and structures is under an eschatological tension. That is, the present order of human society, as God created and intended it to exist as part of the world order, is "good." There is no intrinsic evil embedded in the created order, nor is the created order to be despised as unworthy of our attention. Christians sometimes forget this, and make the mistake of thinking that the "business" of the world is basically evil and therefore cannot be "of God."

Put in terms of the "business" of managing Christian organizations, this negative and pessimistic view of the created order would tend to spiritualize the management of Christian organizations and substitute prayer for planning and faith for forecasting. But this is wrong. The spiritual task of managing Christian organizations is first of all a task of managing an organization with full responsibility for its participation in the created structure of this world as God intended it.

This is why the apostle Paul suggested that at least one important qualification for the spiritual leadership of the church was that one should first have demonstrated competence in "managing a household" (1 Tim. 3:12) and not be "profligate" (Titus 1:6). In Paul's eyes, managing a household and managing one's resources well is a mark of being a good "business person." Even though all of this "business" will pass away in the end, that which will exist ultimately for the glory of God (when "heaven and earth have passed away") is the people of God.

The created cosmos is intended to serve as an environment of space and time for the preparation of human society to be the people of God. The organizational structures and functions of society can be called into the service of that preparation.

There is, to be sure, an inherent tension of a positive nature between the structures of human society as a created order and the ultimate form of the people of God. This is the beginning of a theological critique of human society and organizations. The doctrine of creation, which flows out of the covenant purpose of God for his people, teaches us that all created social structures (organizations) can serve as a provisional means to the ultimate end, which God determined beforehand to exist eternally for his glory.

In concluding our analysis of the first thesis, we can form a diagram of what we have been saying (see Figure 3, p. 24). One should always read this figure from right to left, from the ultimate order to the present order. This illustrates our claim that the priority in theological reflection is to think out of the creative Word of God as the original and ultimate source of all created reality. The cosmos (on the extreme left) represents the created order, with society, organization, and management all part of the created order. On the extreme right, we

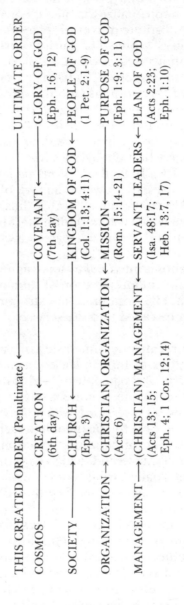

THIS CREATED ORDER (Penultimate) ⟶ ULTIMATE ORDER

COSMOS ⟶ CREATION ⟶ GLORY OF GOD
(6th day)   (Eph. 1:6, 12)

SOCIETY ⟶ CHURCH ⟶ KINGDOM OF GOD ← PEOPLE OF GOD
(Eph. 3)   (Col. 1:13; 4:11)   (1 Pet. 2:1-9)

ORGANIZATION → (CHRISTIAN) ORGANIZATION ← MISSION ⟶ PURPOSE OF GOD
(Acts 6)   (Rom. 15:14-21)   (Eph. 1:9; 3:11)

MANAGEMENT ⟶ (CHRISTIAN) MANAGEMENT ⟵ SERVANT LEADERS ← PLAN OF GOD
(Acts 13; 15;   (Isa. 48:17;   (Acts 2:23;
Eph. 4; 1 Cor. 12;14) Heb. 13:7, 17)   Eph. 1:10)

Figure 3

see that all things are created for the glory of God, which is the ultimate or final order. Also part of the ultimate order are the people of God, the purpose of God, and the plan of God.

Read in this way, with the cosmos coming out of the ultimate order, we can understand the cosmos as creation only if we first come to understand God's covenant as enacted through his election of Israel. Remember that the Exodus from Egypt and the making of the covenant occurred *before* the writing of the creation account in Genesis! It was during the Exodus that God gave Moses the divine commandment that established the seventh day as the last day of the week—the day of rest. The story of creation is thus written from the perspective of the "end" (seventh day), not the beginning. The seventh day as the last day has a priority over the sixth day, which is the penultimate day. The sixth day, then, is a concept that stands for creation (the penultimate), while the seventh day stands for covenant (the ultimate).

Is this confusing? Well it is when we begin our thinking from our place in the cosmos, where everything occurs from "first to last." In theological reflection, however, we must reverse this kind of thinking, so to speak. Our point of entry here is actually "in the middle" rather than at either the beginning or the end. Thus, the second column from the right is the point at which we enter into theological reflection. The covenant with Israel had a historical beginning, and led to a doctrine of creation as well as to an understanding of God as the "Glorious One." The kingdom of God occurs within the created order in at least a provisional way as God's rule over his people. From this perspective, one can understand that human society takes form as the church on the one hand, and as the people of God in the ultimate order. Likewise, the purpose of God comes into the created order through mission, and mission transforms organization into Christian organization. The servant leaders disclose the plan of God and transform management into Christian management.

Remember, this exercise in theological reflection has been for the purpose of establishing the first thesis, that the present world order, including human society with its organizational structure, was originally designed by God, the Creator and Lord. It is therefore "good" when it is understood as God originally intended it, even though provisional and temporal.

It can be and is meant to be used as the environment where "preparation" is made for the ultimate. It is the sixth day, the penultimate day, in which preparation is made for the seventh day.

All created things are provisional to the extent that they are destined to disintegrate with the eventual passing away of this world and all that is in it. This includes the organizations and institutions human beings create as well as material objects. However, our point here is that God has created this present world, provisional though it is, to be what it is. It is to be good insofar as it is used and developed for the purpose for which God created it, and as a place of preparation for the seventh day.

But—some will protest—all is not well in this created order: it has fallen into sin and therefore is no longer a good order. So it has. But here we must be careful, for God has not abandoned his created order to its fallen state. We are now ready for our second thesis.

> *Thesis 2.* The existing cosmos has suffered a radical disorder that cannot be renewed through the natural world itself; this disorder alienates both social and cosmic structures of creation from their created order and destiny.

Starting in the middle, as we suggested above, places us in a fallen world, not in the original paradise. At this point some would object. "All of this talk about the created order being good is nonsense. Human society is poisoned by greed, human organizations exist to serve this greed, and management principles are godless and unethical." These are strong words, and not totally inaccurate as a description of much of modern society. But I happen to think that we know how bad it really is only when we know how good it is meant to be. Therefore, we dare not look at the fallenness of the created order outside of the framework of the whole. That is, we must remember to look at the penultimate through the lens of the ultimate. Or, to put it another way, to look at the sixth day through the window of the seventh day.

Let's look at a schematic diagram created out of Figure 3 with the additional factor of humankind's fall into sin.

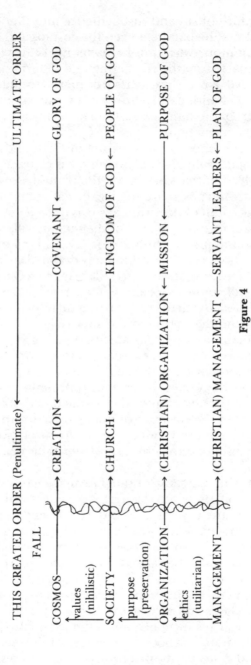

Figure 4

The entrance of sin and disobedience into the world God created shatters the bond between the cosmos and God's creation. What is more, when this happens, not only is the cosmos wrenched apart from the sustaining and determining power of the creative Word, but a fissure opens up that alienates human society—with its structures of organization and management—from the ultimate order. Human society no longer is a sign of the formation of a people of God; human organizations no longer embody the purpose of God; and the enterprise of human management no longer is characterized by a servant leadership that carries out the plan of God.

It is not my purpose here to give a treatise on sin. I accept the biblical account of the original sin as depicted in Genesis 3 not only as a spiritual defection of the human will but also as a fatal infection that turns human society, with all of its structures, into a "homeless" and ultimately doomed existence. It is not too much to say that with this fall away from God's creative Word and will, human society is torn from its roots in the kingdom of God—with the result that it turns in on itself with a desperation and determination to survive at all costs.

What happens to the basic values God has given to the cosmos through its covenantal orientation to the Creator when it suffers alienation through the Fall? There are still values, to be sure. But now the values the cosmos represents are nihilistic. The cosmos is passing away and is doomed to destruction. All values rooted in the cosmos are finally linked with the materialist and reductionist view of reality. No idea or ideal can be sustained in light of the eventual and inevitable disintegration of the cosmos.

What happens to a sense of purpose in human society when that society collapses into itself? Like values, which become nihilistic when the cosmos is considered an end in itself, purpose in human social endeavor becomes linked with motives of preservation. As a result, self-preservation and self-determination become institutionalized into the very core of society and its structures.

What happens to the basic ethical structure of a society when its purposes and values are directed finally toward the cosmos? Ethical instincts become utilitarian and pragmatic. When the purpose of a society is basically to preserve its own existence and to insure its own future, moral values tend to be bent toward the service of survival. It then becomes expedient to sacrifice the individual to the good of the organization and to offer up the humanity of the organization as a sacrifice on the altar of institutional survival.

The religious establishment in Jesus' day made just this assessment when his popularity and power were considered to be subversive to the institutional goal of survival. Caiaphas, who was the high priest, told his "management team," "You know nothing at all; you do not understand that it is expedient for you that one man should die for the people, and that the whole nation should not perish" (John 11:49-50).

Is it not quite clear, as Figure 4 shows, that the effect of the Fall is devastating to the whole structure of human organizations? And does it not then follow that the management of these organizations will be hopelessly determined by a movement toward preservation that ultimately is voided by the nihilism intrinsic to the cosmos separated from God? That which was penultimate as a created order must now create its own ultimate. In fact, the very cosmos itself becomes the ultimate and experiences what the apostle Paul described so eloquently in his letter to the church at Rome: "They exchanged the truth about God for a lie and worshiped and served the creature rather than the Creator" (Rom. 1:25).

In God's original order, the cosmos and human society, including its organizational structures, are provisional, and as such have a provisional value as created structures that serve to glorify God. With the Fall, that which was provisional now seeks to become an absolute measure of its own value and the final end of its own striving. There is no longer any seventh day for the cosmos. The sixth day has become the end in itself and swallows up the energies and efforts of all that lives. As the apostle has written:

> For the creation waits with eager longing for the revealing of the sons of God; for the creation was subjected to futility, not of its own will but by the will of him who subjected it in hope; because the creation itself will be set free from its bondage to decay and obtain the glorious liberty of the children of God. We know that the whole creation has been groaning in travail together until now. (Rom. 8:19-22)

In our second thesis we have attempted to show the effect of the theological construct of sin and the Fall upon human society and its organizational structures. We must remember, however, that the cosmos, human society, and its organizational structures are not intrinsically evil. They only become evil when estranged and alienated from God's creative Word and purpose. Therefore, we can portray God's redemption as a restoration of the cosmos and the created structures of human society to their intended status and purpose.

This is important. We must recognize that a Christian organization is not a substitute for the organizational structure of the created world, but it is the way in which human society can be brought back under the mandate of its original creation and be oriented toward God's ultimate purpose—which, as we have seen, is to form a people for himself to share in his eternal glory. When we speak of the mandate of creation, we are referring to God's command to the first human persons, that they should "subdue" the earth and "have dominion" over all things in the earth (Gen. 1:28). Christian organizations are not excused from this mandate.

We are now ready to bring the theological construct of redemption into the discussion, and we will do this by introducing the third thesis.

Thesis 3. Through God's intervention by the giving of his Word, first of all to Israel as his new order of humanity, and finally through Jesus Christ as the new humanity, both human society and the cosmos are brought back under the creation mandate.

The theological term *incarnation* is derived from the biblical account of the birth of Jesus as written by the apostle John: "The Word became flesh and dwelt among us" (John 1:14). The Latin word for "flesh" is *carnis,* and the Latin translation of the Greek "became flesh" is literally *incarnatio.* From this, we derive the English word *incarnation.* As used in this discussion, *incarnation* includes the entire history of the birth, death, and resurrection of Christ. We believe that through the incarnation God sent his only Son to take upon himself the humanity of Adam, brought under the curse of sin and death through the Fall, so that he might restore humanity to its original and ultimate destiny to share the eternal glory of God.

Because sin and the resulting Fall tore human society, including all of its structures, apart from its orientation to the purpose of God, the incarnation of God into human flesh goes as deep as sin does. This means that the incarnation can be seen as the divine provision by which cosmos can be restored to its status as a created order, human society can be restored to the status of being the people of God, and the organizational structures and management functions of society can be used to work out God's purpose and plan. This is depicted in Figure 5.

As the Incarnate One, Jesus is, in his own words, the one who "has come from above." But he is also the one who took upon himself the same nature of flesh and blood that fallen sinners have in order that he might deliver those who were subject to bondage (Heb. 2:14-15). Therefore the incarnation is depicted in Figure 5 on the side of the ultimate order, on the one hand, but also fully within the created order on the other hand. This is what we meant earlier in this chapter (Figure 1) when we referred to Jesus as the "essential link" between the ultimate order and the created order.

It is through the incarnation of the creative and creating Word, Jesus Christ, that God initiates the reconciliation of the world to himself. This act of reconciliation is meant also to restore the created order to its true purpose of preparing a people for God's own eternal glory. This act of reconciliation, which becomes the good news or gospel of salvation, is not first of all an idea or an ideal form of humanity. Rather, it is first of all an embodiment, an assumption of human, creaturely flesh on the part of the divine Son of God. The incarnation, and the gospel it offers as liberation from bondage and restoration to God's eternal purpose, thus is part of the very structure of the reality of this world. In fact, one cannot know the world and its own structures for what it really is without knowing it as grasped by God through the act of reconciliation in Christ. What the world knows as reality is actually now unreality in light of God's reality.

What happens when the value of God's covenant love is actually worked back into the cosmos through incarnation? The cosmos finds its own destiny of "nothingness" (nihilism)

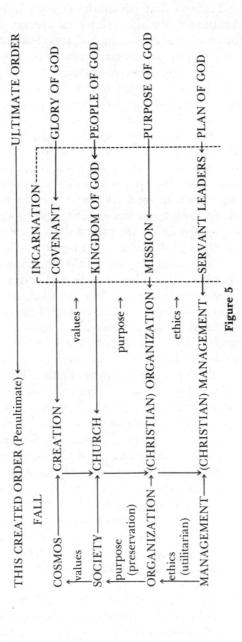

Figure 5

THIS CREATED ORDER (Penultimate) ←————— ULTIMATE ORDER

FALL

COSMOS ————→ CREATION ————————————————→ GLORY OF GOD

↓values   values →

SOCIETY ————→ CHURCH ←——————————————— KINGDOM OF GOD ←— PEOPLE OF GOD

↓purpose   purpose →
(preservation)

ORGANIZATION —→ (CHRISTIAN) ORGANIZATION ←— MISSION ←——————— PURPOSE OF GOD

↓ethics   ethics →
(utilitarian)

MANAGEMENT ———→ (CHRISTIAN) MANAGEMENT ←— SERVANT LEADERS ←— PLAN OF GOD

INCARNATION

brought under judgment and the true value of existing for the glory of God brought back into view. The Psalmist anticipates this when he sings: "The heavens are telling the glory of God; and the firmament proclaims his handiwork" (Ps. 19:1). Here we see that the values inherent in the comos and all of its structures are created values; values "created out of nothing," if you please, in order that God may be glorified in his creation.

What happens when the kingdom of God actually comes into the midst of human society with its liberating and life-giving power? Here we see that the purpose of a human society is diverted from the fatal project of self-preservation and turned, instead, toward the purpose of building the community. Now the church emerges not only as the "body of Christ" but also as the "re-formation" of human society into a people of God as a sign of the kingdom of God, pointing ultimately to an ultimate existence as the people who share in God's eternal glory.

What happens when the organizational structure of society is brought under the purpose of God as enacted through the mission of Christ in the world? Christian organizations emerge as the new ethical motivation of a society where ethics are delivered from the impersonal and dehumanizing tactics of expediency and the utilitarian motives of institutional survival. Jesus exemplified this quite dramatically when he brought a new ethical imperative into the institutional, organized legalism of the Jewish religion: "The sabbath was made for man, not man for the sabbath" (Mark 2:27).

What happens when the leadership function of management comes under the mandate of the mission of God as set forth in the world through incarnation? Management now becomes the servant of God's purpose and plan, and no longer is in the relentless grip of the utilitarian and self-preservationist drive of organizations under the determinism of the Fall. Under the Lordship of Christ, a new form of leadership emerges called servant leadership. Its goal is not serving the organization's own ethics and purposes, but leading the organization to fulfill God's purpose as a servant of God.

I have attemped, in discussing the third thesis, to show how the radical effect of sin and the Fall has been more radically overcome through the incarnation of God in Jesus Christ.

Therefore, we can now understand the nature and function of Christian organizations in the larger framework of a doctrine of creation and a doctrine of salvation.

One final thesis is a way of bringing to a close our theological discussion.

> *Thesis 4.* This present world and social order, though under the power of the new and creative order established through Jesus Christ, continues to suffer a tension between the new and old order. This present and continuing ministry of Jesus Christ takes place through the provisional forms of the church and its organizations as a sign of the kingdom of God.

In our development of a theological framework within which we can understand the nature and function of Christian organizations, we recognized two basic tensions existing between this present order and the ultimate order. The first tension was said to be a positive one by which the created order is constantly reminded that it is not ultimate but rather penultimate. This tension allows the created order, with its social and organizational structures, to have a reality of its own. However, this reality is provisional and not eternal; it is contingent upon the power that created it and sustains it. Thus, this created order is "good" and capable of serving the good purpose of the Creator.

However, with the entrance of sin into the created order through the presumptuous claim of the first human persons to be "like God," the created order fell away from the ultimate order and fell under the determinism and nihilism that is the inevitable end of the cosmos left to itself. The Creator God, not willing to allow his creation to fall into ruin, now revealed himself as a Redeemer God, summoning the creation back to its original orientation upon the Creator as its ultimate meaning. Through the calling of Israel to be a sign of the kingdom of God and the re-creation of a people of God, and through the incarnation of God in human form, the created order is brought back under the sovereign will and purpose of God. This is the second tension that exists between the created order and the ultimate order.

Many Christians confuse these two tensions, assuming that

the tension between the created order and the Creator is basically a negative one, by which the form and structures of the
created order are evil and incapable of participating in the
work of God. In this view, redemption is a rejection of the
created world and its social and organizational structures.
Such a view, however, tends to absolutize the distinction between the created order and the redeemed order. In the
thinking of those who hold this view, Christian organizations
should not use "worldly" methods to carry out the work of the
kingdom of God. These people are fond of quoting the Scripture that says, "Do not love the world or the things of the
world. . . . For all that is in the world, the lust of the flesh and
the lust of the eyes and the pride of life, is not of the Father but
is of the world" (1 John 2:15-16).

A Christian organization, as defined by those who hold this
negative view of the created order, ought to be spiritual rather
than worldly. This ordinarily means depending upon faith in
God for providing resources for the mission of God rather
than upon the methods and resources of the world. Thus, they
consider more appropriate, if not more spiritual, those dona-
tions that arrive at their headquarters through answers to
prayer rather than through direct mail solicitation. One must
assume that in such cases the actual delivery of the check
through the "worldly" function of the government postal system somehow is sanctified by the prayer as well!

Management of Christian organizations, as those who hold
this pessimistic view of worldly organizations understand it, is
often prefaced by assurances that "God is really the manager
of this organization" and the person in charge is merely his
assistant. Long-range planning is seen as usurping the role of
the Holy Spirit; cost accounting and budget balancing are under suspicion as lack of trust in God; performance evaluations
of employees are taken to be a violation of the "Christian
spirit" in which we all are trying to "serve the Lord."

But perhaps most typical of those Christian organizations
which lean toward this view is the inability to balance the
human factor with the spiritual factor in identifying the goals
of the organization with the mission of the organization. Because the mission is directly related to the kingdom of God, its
goals do not easily include the personal, human, and social
factors of those who are involved in the organizations. The

personal and family life of managers are too often neglected
or even destroyed by the "messianic" demands of the organization. By implication, if not by organizational policy, one is
expected to sacrifice personal goals for institutional goals, and
to accept marginal economic and professional compensation
for services rendered, because such seeking after gain is
"worldly"—and besides, this is the Lord's work and he will
provide his own reward to his workers!

I realize that I have caricatured and exaggerated such
forms of Christian organizations, but I did so only to make a
point. It is unbiblical to confuse the positive and creative tension that belongs to the created order with the negative tension
that was introduced by sin and the Fall. The apostle Paul, no
stranger to the task of leading a mission, knew this quite well.
In his pastoral instructions to Timothy he wrote: "For everything created by God is good, and nothing is to be rejected if it
is received with thanksgiving; for then it is consecrated by the
word of God and prayer" (1 Tim. 4:4).

There is, to be sure, a point of absolute contradiction between a world (cosmos) that has fallen out of its orientation
upon God as Creator and Lord and the ultimate order. But it
was this contradiction that was brought under judgment and
put to death on the cross, not the created order itself. The
incarnation served to link up once again the creative Word
with the created order, to bring it into subjection to the
Creator.

Through Jesus Christ, all that belongs to the penultimate
order—the cosmos, human society, and its organizations—has
been brought under both the judgment and the grace of God.
What is brought under judgment is the self-serving motives
and nihilistic values of the created order. As the one who
fulfills the covenant, Jesus works this covenant back into the
cosmos as a gracious doctrine of creation, liberating the cosmos to testify once again to the glory of God. As the one who
brings the kingdom of God in power, Jesus liberates human
persons from bondage and enslavement to the hopeless destiny of living and dying within the sixth day. As the one who
creates community through his own loving relationship with
the Father, shared with those who become his disciples, Jesus
reaches into the very organizational structures of society with
his ethic of love and releases ethics from captivity to systems of

self-preservation and utilitarianism. And through the giving of the Holy Spirit, who carries the very presence and Spirit of Jesus himself, principles and practices of management and leadership are now liberated to serve the building up of community and fulfilling the will and work of God, for his glory.

Even as the original human society was determined by God to be the "priest of all creation" and responds to God's Word with praise and love, so the new people of God created through the life, death, and resurrection of Jesus Christ are meant to serve as agents of reconciliation by which the cosmos itself is re-ordered in its relation to God the Creator.

This community of reconciliation is the connecting link between gospel and mission under the apostolic mandate. It is also the connecting link between mission and gospel under the theological mandate, by which it reflects back on the gospel so as to prevent mission from losing its orientation to the gospel by sinking too deeply into the ethos of the fallen world.

This community of reconciliation is the church, in its parochial and paraparochial forms. As such, it is the body of Christ, the custodian of both the mandate of creation and the mandate of redemption. Remember, we have spoken earlier of the creation mandate as the command of God given at creation, and said that Christian organizations are not excused from this mandate. The mandate of redemption is the apostolic mandate understood as the gospel imperative to go into all the world as Christ's agents of reconciliation. Christian organizations, as paraparochial forms of the church, are under the same double mandate as the parochial form of the church. Both are signs of the kingdom of God. The uniqueness of Christian organizations vis-à-vis the church in its parochial form, therefore, is not that the former is less a sign of the kingdom than the latter, but that the Christian organization, by definition, carries the mission of the gospel beyond the gathered congregation (parish); thus, the Christian organization is paraparochial rather than parochial in its basic nature and function.

The Christian organization by intention is ordinarily either service and/or product specific, but ordinarily not parish or community specific. That is, it does not intend to replace the parochial function and responsibility of the church as a gathered congregation, though it will not hesitate to fulfill

those functions and this role whenever it is urgent and appropriate that it do so.

The church as a gathered community (parish) assumes,
more or less, an unlimited liability on behalf of its members, in
being a sign of the kingdom of God. In its paraparochial form,
however, the church assumes those responsibilities (liabilities)
that are more appropriate to its own nature and purpose as a
mission of Christ. It is in this sense that a Christian organization might be said to have a "limited liability" with respect to its
members. However, this can be said only with some caution
and qualification. We must also understand that the members
of a Christian organization are rooted in a gathered congregation (parish) where an unlimited liability for each member is
assumed. I am not suggesting that Christian organizations
have no responsibility for the personal welfare of their members. There must exist what one might call a "symbiotic relation" between the parochial and paraparochial form of the
church.

Let me suggest an example of a "limited liability" type of
situation. A member of a Christian organization suffers a family tragedy, perhaps a death or an accident. The Christian
organization responds out of love and concern for a fellow
Christian, and extends its resources of Christian community
so far as is possible within its own mission-specific task. There
may be need for pastoral counseling, a diaconal ministry to the
family, a service of comfort and hope at the graveside. This is
the responsibility, ordinarily, of a gathered congregation with
respect to its members. The ministry of the paraparochial
form of the church will be Christian-to-Christian, not usually a
function of the staff or line relationships of the organization.

What about the case where an employee of a Christian organization is to be released, either because of a failure to function
in accordance with the task specifications, or due to necessary
cutbacks of the staff? The liability of a Christian organization
toward its employees is limited by certain contractual understandings. Painful though it may be, Christian employees may
have to be counseled out of a task (obviously a euphemism for
being fired!). However, this should not be handled in an un-
Christian manner, and it will become the diaconal responsibility of the parochial form of the church to step in and continue
to minister to the person's needs. For this reason, the para-

parochial form of the church and the parochial form need to
be closely aligned, with the common denominator being the
individual.

Christian organizations, therefore, not only share in the
creation mandate and the redemptive mandate, but also in the
"ecclesial" mandate—that of being a form of the church as the
body of Christ. This ecclesial mandate not only brings the
paraparochial organization under the responsibility of being
"the church," but it also means that members and leaders of
Christian organizations can be encouraged to seek and be af-
firmed as having "Christ's gifts to his church" (Eph. 4:7,
11-13). Christian organizations have all of the resources of
spiritual empowerment, as well as accountability to Christ
himself, that belong to the church as a sign of the kingdom of
God.

Because Christian organizations are under the mandate *to
be* Christian, not only to have members who are Christians, the
organization itself can and must experience the impact of the
Word of God and the Holy Spirit. Because Christian organizations also experience Christian community in their organizational life and function, they must exhibit the ethical mandate
of demonstrating love in relationships as well as in mission.
Because Christian organizations are under the mandate of
theological reflection, an understanding of biblical teachings
and principles is essential to each component of the organization's life and practice.

Therefore, as Thesis 4 states it, "this present and continuing ministry of Jesus Christ takes place through the provisional forms of the church and its organizations as a sign of the
kingdom of God." The incarnation of the Word into human
flesh and the atonement from sin on the cross are much more
than technical theological doctrines. What is involved is God's
work of reconciliation—that is his business. Reconciliation as
the work of God is the good news of the gospel. But it is also the
mission of the church as it penetrates the fallen and alienated
structures of human society and seeks to create new structures
that liberate human persons from sin, despair, and im-
poverishment of life. A Christian organization is a sign of the
kingdom of God to the extent that it is a community of reconciliation under the authority of God's Word and is "minding
God's business" of reconciliation.

Reconciliation reverses the nihilism that can force leadership and management to end up serving the causes of self-preservation and utilitarianism. Now that God has grasped the world again through the incarnation, the cosmos itself is given the promise of liberation from its bondage (Rom. 8:20, 23). But the cosmos does not experience this liberation independently of the liberation and reconciliation of human society. And this reconciliation does not take place through a spiritual "implant" where only "souls are saved," but through the very structures of human society and by means of the organizations that now are called into being as servants of this redemptive goal.

We now need to assess whether or not this chapter has lived up to its promise. We had set forth three purposes and promised to answer several questions. Two of the three purposes have been addressed quite specifically. We have attempted to show how Christian organizations are part of the church as God's covenant people, and we have attempted to show how the management of Christian organizations relates to the creative and redemptive purpose of God. We did this through a discussion of the two mandates (creation and redemption) and by showing that there is both a positive and a negative tension between the created and ultimate order. The third purpose, that of describing the leadership function of Christian organizations in light of God's will, we have only alluded to indirectly; we will discuss it more fully in the next chapter.

In sum, let's review the answers to questions that have been raised about the nature and function of Christian organizations.

1. Christian organizations that are paraparochial in nature are, as a form of the church, signs of the kingdom of God.

2. Christian organizations have a "limited liability" with respect to their members; members enter into contractual relations with the organization; Christian organizations may also constitute a "Christian community" on an informal basis, but this community does not replace the parochial community as the gathered congregation.

3. Christian organizations make use of principles and practices of management drawn out of the created social structure; that which makes the management of Christian organizations

Christian is the liberation of management principles and practices from the self-serving and utilitarian ends that belong to the fallen world.

4. The incarnation of God in Christ affirms the structures of the created social order as good insofar as they are directed toward the spiritual end of participating in the ultimate glory of God; managing "God's business" is a task that takes place in the world, not in a "spiritual vacuum."

5. The goals and values of Christian organizations warrant the survival of these organizations as business enterprises to the extent that they effectively carry out the mission of Christ in the world; effectiveness, not merely efficiency, is the criterion Christian organizations use to evaluate success; this evaluation is also a process of theological reflection.

6. Christian organizations may be viewed as "preparing the way of the Lord"; all methods used to manage Christian organizations will be validated insofar as they serve as preparation of the way.

And so we have come to the end of the matter. Theological reflection does require that we "gird up our loins," as Job was urged to do. And perhaps in the end we need to remember that Job also confessed, when his suffering was over:

> Therefore I have uttered what I did not understand,
> things too wonderful for me, which I did not know.
> (Job 42:3)

CHAPTER THREE

MANAGEMENT, MEGATRENDS, AND METHODS

The story is told of a farmer in South Dakota who was visited by the county agricultural agent, who sought to convince the farmer that he could increase his production by using more modern methods. The agricultural specialist argued that a better system of crop rotation and soil management, including proven methods of applied herbicides and insecticides, would result in greater yields of grain.

The farmer was not convinced. The county agent pleaded, "But I can show you new methods of farming that will make you the envy of all of your neighbors!"

"Shucks," the farmer replied, "I ain't farming now half as good as I know how."

There it is—the primal clash between the technician and the traditionalist: the eternal standoff between the "how to" and the "want to." Don't get me wrong. It is not that our farmer friend does not have visions of bumper crops that are the envy of his neighbors. It is not that he does not dream of the one "good year" in which all debts can be paid off. No, he is a dreamer of dreams and a seer of visions. Unfortunately, his methods are attached to the routine repetition of yesterday's habits while his dreams and visions are surrendered to the "will of the gods" who control with capricious unpredictability the elements of nature. Thus, the crops may fail, but he cannot really fail as a manager of the crops.

This, then, is the crux of the matter. How do we really connect our management of Christian organizations with the "will of God"? How do we disengage our methods from bondage to what has always been in order to make them the servants of imagination, of hope, of the future? Is it enough to be jarred out of complacency by a quick reading of *Megatrends*? Or should we send out for a management consultant who will administer a "quick fix" to our organizational structure and tell us to buy a computer? Has anyone designed a software package that programs the will of God?

I am not yet convinced that futurology has replaced theology as a way to discover and practice the will of God. Nor am I content, like the farmer, to resist new methods and struggle along "half as good as I know how." What I am looking for is a perspective on the managing of Christian organizations by which methods can be developed as the servant of goals and objectives that embody the will of God.

As we have seen, Christian organizations by nature serve a purpose that originates in God's creative and redemptive will. God's will for human society is that it fulfill his covenant purpose and promise here on earth and be prepared to be a "people of God" destined to share his eternal glory. The will of God is expressed in a community that lives under God's rule and so becomes a sign of the kingdom of God. This community, the church, seeks to bring the "gospel of the kingdom" to all of human society, liberating the world from its fateful bondage to self-serving strivings and healing its estrangement from God's gracious purpose and promise.

Thus, the church in its parochial form becomes the "gathered congregation" of those who have received the good news of the gospel and have been baptized into Christ, becoming already a people of God being prepared to share in God's eternal life and glory. However, the will of God is not merely that the church should grow as the community of Christ, but that it should go as the servant of Christ to all the world, carrying out the apostolic mandate of the gospel.

Christian organizations, as we have defined them, are the paraparochial forms of the church's mission and ministry of the gospel. As such, they seek to carry out God's will, revealed through his covenant purpose and promise and made final and complete through Jesus Christ. While each Christian organization has a discrete purpose and mission of its own, it does not have a will of its own. Rather, these organizations exist to fulfill God's purpose in the world and to embody his will in their own purposes and actions.

Those who manage Christian organizations, therefore, are under the mandate to lead the organization in this direction. This requires a continual activity of theological reflection to be sure that we are "minding *God's* business"!

In this chapter I hope to give managers of Christian organizations a perspective on management by which the immediate objectives of the organization can be related to the ultimate objective of preparing the way for the kingdom of God.

Typically, we are taught to assume that correct methods will lead to a desired outcome. By "method" we mean a process, technique, or structure of organization by which an organization invests its resources and energies in order to reach a desired outcome. Because this desired outcome is an immediate objective, the methods can become quite pragmatic. A correct method is one that reaches the immediate objective with the greatest efficiency in the expenditure of resources and energies.

For example, if a Christian organization defines its mission as the task of feeding the starving children in Africa, and identifies its resources as the free-will offerings of Christians, the task of managing that organization will be to determine the most effective methods of raising money and distributing food in Africa. Can we assume that, because it most certainly is God's will that starving children be fed, the most efficient methods of soliciting contributions and distributing the food are the will of God for that organization? Is there only one correct method? George Mueller, of Bristol, England, insisted that faith and prayer were the most effective methods to accomplish this goal, and suggested that this was God's method. World Vision International, on the other hand, uses a computerized mailing list to accomplish the same goal, but on a much larger scale. Is one method spiritual and the other worldly?

How do managers of Christian organizations lead the organization to reflect upon its methods in terms of biblical principles and ultimate values? How do these managers understand their own role in leading an organization to carry out the work of the kingdom of God on earth in such a way that God is glorified in heaven? Perhaps, with the apostle Paul, we should cry out, "Who is sufficient for these things?" (2 Cor. 2:16). But then we should also have to say with him that *we* are, "for we are not, like so many, peddlers of God's word; but as men of sincerity, as commissioned by God, in the sight of God we speak in Christ" (2 Cor. 2:17).

Let us therefore try for the perspective.

Christian organizations—as all organizations in this created order—exist with some form of social structure and form. It is, however, the nature of Christian organizations to know that this created order is subject to ultimate ends not intrinsic to the natural order itself. Rather, the created and natural order is subject to the purpose and promise of the Creator. It is also the nature of Christian organizations to know that the social structure of the organization is part of the created order in which human persons are determined by the original and creative Word of God to be the people of God. Further, it is the nature of Christian organizations to know that Jesus Christ, as the incarnation of that original creative Word of God, is the presence and power of the kingdom of God in the midst of this created order and perverse disorder.

We need to be reminded here of a critical point made earlier when we discussed the relation between the ultimate order and the created order (see Figure 3, p. 24). The movement of theological reflection is always from the ultimate toward the penultimate, from the last toward the next to the last; that is, from the perspective of God's covenant purpose and promise toward creation. This direction cannot be reversed. The ultimate gives meaning and order to the penultimate; the covenant gives meaning and purpose to creation.

The ultimate, in coming into the penultimate, does not destroy the penultimate, even though the penultimate is now relative and no longer holds absolute power over human nature and destiny. As Dietrich Bonhoeffer put it, "We now know the final [ultimate] Word. God has spoken it through Jesus Christ. We are justified by faith through his blood by grace."[1] However, the ultimate Word does not destroy the value of the penultimate experience of this created order. The ultimate informs the penultimate of its true nature, purpose, value, and ethical responsibility. Because Jesus Christ belongs to this present time as well as to the future time, Christian organizations can exist in the present in good conscience, tak-

---

1. D. Bonhoeffer, *Ethics* (New York: Macmillan, 1955), p. 121.

ing with full seriousness the need and concerns of the people
for whom God sent his Son.

To quote Bonhoeffer again, "The hungry man needs bread
and the homeless man needs a roof. The dispossessed need
justice and the lonely need fellowship. The undisciplined need
order and the slave needs freedom."[2] There is no warrant for
using the ultimate purpose of God as an excuse to evade his
purpose and will within this penultimate time. However, the
form of Christ's ministry in this present order is that of "preparing the way" for the kingdom of God. Thus, Bonhoeffer
argued, the strategies by which we seek to fulfill the will of God
in this present time must not depend so much upon "methods" as upon "preparing the way" for the kingdom of God.[3]

It appears to me that this is a helpful insight in our attempt
to gain a perspective for managing Christian organizations.
Methods cannot of themselves bring in the kingdom. The
kingdom, however, brings in methods as appropriate means
to accomplish the work of the kingdom. If, in fact, a Christian
organization uses methods derived from sociological, psycho-
logical, and economic principles and practices in order to advance the purpose of the organization, these methods must
come under the critique of "preparing the way of the Lord."
Or to put it another way, if these methods are not capable of
being used in the service of the ultimate nature and purpose of
God for his people, they are not valid.

There are two points to be made here. First, methods do not
have the power in and of themselves to fulfill the kingdom of
God or to move from an immediate objective to an ultimate
objective. Even as one cannot move out of created structures
into uncreated structures and realities, one cannot by virtue of
the "right method" move an organization into the future of
the kingdom of God. Second, methods are neutral, not inherently good or evil. While an evil purpose can devise methods
that work evil, a method, as a process, technique, or structure
of organization, has the power to create neither good nor evil.

The function of management for a Christian organization,
therefore, takes place under the mandate of the ultimate purpose of God through Jesus Christ, and in a style and manner

2. Ibid., p. 137.
3. Ibid., p. 141.

that serves the purposes of the gospel. To speak of "Christian management" in the sense that certain management principles or methods are inherently Christian would be a dubious approach, in my judgment. However, there may well be distinctively Christian approaches to the use of management principles and methods that are determined by the nature and purpose of Christian organizations.

Managers of Christian organizations will now be aware of the tension that exists between the ultimate and the penultimate, that is expressed in every aspect of the nature and purpose of the organization. The present world structure, with all of its various forms and structures, is part of the heaven and earth that is passing away. That which is created not only has a beginning, it has an end. But the end is not a "telos" or final purpose that is realized through the created order itself. Rather, the end is the "eschaton," the Day of the Lord. This final Word of God has entered into the present order as a judgment (it is passing away) as well as an affirmation of God's intention for his creation (the Word of the Lord abides forever). God's final purpose is realized and given by way of promise in the "seventh day"—the ultimate day. The "sixth day" of creation has no ultimate promise or possibility given to it except that it stands under the sovereign power and grace of the seventh day. However, the sixth day, as God's created order, continues to be the arena in which the Word of God comes to expression as a witness and summons to enter into the seventh day, the day of God's eternal rest and glory.

Christian organizations must understand this tension and be willing to participate in the formation of the gospel in this present world without making a false dichotomy between the spiritual and the worldly. The created order, which God affirms as good, can be used with good conscience to the extent that we recognize it as the penultimate and not the ultimate order. Also, it can be used to the extent that we bring under judgment the methods and structures of evil, so that the world can be liberated to serve the purpose and promise of God. Out of this creative tension emerge the values, purposes, ethical criteria, and management and leadership principles that are appropriate to the nature and function of Christian organizations.

These values, purposes, and ethical criteria are not alien to the cosmos and to human society as determined by the originally creative Word of God. Therefore, in a world order that is upheld and sustained in relation to God as Creator, there will be no conflict between the values and purposes of human society and the kingdom of God. For the Creator did not give the cosmos its own values and purposes in such a way that it could exist autonomously with respect to God. Those values and purposes God originally gave to the created order really do belong to that order, though it cannot know this apart from the Creator's continual act of revelation, which comes in the form of a covenant purpose and promise.

Let us pursue this line of thought a bit further. As we have said, the task of managing Christian organizations is to embody the will of God in the organization's mission and function in such a way that the purpose and promise of God comes into the present from the future. By linking purpose with promise we have linked mission with hope and the present with the future. The gospel itself is a gospel of hope to the hopeless and of promise to those who are destitute and forsaken. Therefore, the mission statement of a Christian organization must have as much promise in it as purpose. It must have a perspective by which the present is connected to the future and through which immediate objectives are related to ultimate objectives. For the will of God is not exhausted in reaching an immediate objective as the outworking of the mission of Christ in the world. Strategic planning must include promises as well as purposes and must have a hold on the future as well as a hand on the present.

But how does one plan for the future? How does one get from here to there when no method is capable of bringing in the kingdom?

By now it should be clear that looking at the future from a theological perspective is quite different from looking at it from a worldly perspective. The future, in a theological view, is both a purpose and a promise that has come to the present, rather than being extrapolated out of the present. The content of the future is thus revealed to be the gracious purpose of God himself as the Creator. In other words, the will of God is a coming of the future into the present in the form of an encounter between the present and the future. This is what I mean by saying that the will of God is connected with God's purpose as well as his promise.

To illustrate this difference, let's look at two Latin words that refer to the future. Our English word *future* is derived from the Latin *futurum*, "what will be," or "what may be." The *futurum* arises out of the present and has its potential in the possibilities that emerge out of the present. In this sense of the word, the future cannot really be any more than the extrapolation of the present. Thus, the "future" is already a "future past," because nothing can enter in that is not already present as some possibility. There is indeed "nothing new under the sun" (Eccles. 1:9).

In contrast, the Latin word *adventus* points to that which is "coming to the present." This kind of future does not arise as a possibility out of the present, but rather encounters the present as that which approaches and brings to it a reality not found as a possibility of the present itself. The Latin *adventus* is a translation of the Greek *parousia*, which described the arrival of persons or the occurrence of events that were anticipated but not under the control or power of the present. The New Testament uses the word to describe the arrival of the Messiah and refers directly to the coming of Christ into this world as the "advent" of his presence and the manifestation of God's final purpose and promise for the world (e.g., 2 Thess. 2:1).[4]

The New Testament concept of the future in terms of the advent of the Day of the Lord at Christ's coming is quite different from that of the ancient Greeks. Hesiod described the eternal being of Zeus by saying, "Zeus was and Zeus is and Zeus will be." In contrast, the Book of Revelation says, "Peace from Him who is and who was and who is to come" (1:4). In place of the future tense of the verb *einai*, "to be," we find here the future tense of *erchesthai*, "to come." God's future is not in "what comes to be," but in him "who comes."

In this sense, then, the future is not merely the novel or the unexpected that we are supposed to predict. Neither is the future an extrapolation out of the factors and tendencies of

4. For this discussion of *adventus* and *futurum* I am indebted to an essay by Jürgen Moltmann entitled "Theological Perspectives on the Future," colloquium paper, Lutheran Brotherhood, Houston, Texas, January 29, 1979.

the past and present, as is suggested by the word *futurum*. This concept of the future tends to project trends and signs forward as that which "brings us into the future." Obviously this function of planning and projecting is necessary to a degree in order for an organization to extend its mission and purpose forward into the immediate future. Five- and ten-year plans are helpful devices that enable an organization to transform a mission statement into an effective strategy and task.

However, if the future as that which the will of God leads us toward is also viewed as an "advent" of the promise and presence of God, then we cannot reach or realize this future by method alone. The biblical concept of the way in which this future is anticipated and realized is through "preparation of the way." Originally set forth by the prophet Isaiah as a messianic utterance of comfort and promise (Isa. 40:1-5), the promise was picked up by John the Baptist and uttered again to signal the significance of his own ministry as well as to point toward Jesus as the one who had come to bring this promise into reality (Matt. 3:3).

The following diagram represents this distinction between method and preparation of the way.

PAST——PRESENT————*METHOD*————→ FUTURUM (future)

extrapolation
prognosis
planning/projection

PAST——PRESENT ←——*PREPARATION*——ADVENTUS (future)

anticipation
imagination
reflection/planning

Figure 6

We can see again in the above diagram the perspective that theological reflection brings to the planning process for Christian organizations. By seeking to move from the present to the future through methods, one extrapolates out of the present into the future. The only way in which one can overcome the built-in bias toward preservation of the present is through the introduction of novelty. This can take the form of novel methods, in hopes that new methods alone will bring some new insight or experience, or it can take the form of novel ideas, which are as often conceived out of desperation as out of inspiration.

However, in viewing the future as *adventus,* as that which is coming into the present and is already present, preparation of the way replaces method as the technical process for discovering and implementing the will of God. This has a distinct advantage over the method of extrapolation as a device for planning.

For example, extrapolating out of past experiences and present trends presupposes the existing structures as possibilities for creating and bringing in the future. The realm of what is possible beyond what is presently the case moves from what is determinate into what is indeterminate. The realm of choice now depends upon that which is indeterminate. The more these extrapolations move out of the past (and the present is already the past for the planning process) and move beyond present realities, the more imprecise and speculative they become. The alternative choices then offered tend to be evaluated in terms of how they will affect the present situation. Thus, despite the innovations offered through speculation about the future, methods tend to become conservative and protectionist of the present. This is why ten-year planning documents tend to be ignored in day-to-day operations.

However, please don't misunderstand me at this point. As a process of planning, I believe that extrapolation is a valuable and necessary method. Planning documents that utilize this method should not be ignored because of it. But when the method of extrapolation is virtually the only device used in planning, the plan becomes dissociated from promise and mired down in bureaucracy.

Christian organizations that operate primarily out of the extrapolation method in determining long-range plans tend to bury the will of God in the day-to-day operations of the organization. The organization itself is viewed as "willed into existence" by God, often through the vision and personal energies (charisma) of an entrepreneur founder/leader. The managing of the organization becomes a "method" of accomplishing the vision. Planning becomes extrapolation and projection, with the result that God's will is less invested in the "long-range plan" than it is in the existence of the organization itself. Those who keep the organization alive through day-to-day operations are "doing God's will." Those who make projections and plans are viewed as making unnecessary "busy work" for managers who are already "too busy doing God's business." The Bible is used for devotional and inspirational purposes, to remind the workers and staff that theirs is really a "Christian" organization and therefore is *God's* business.

However, in many such Christian organizations, dramatic changes in direction and even in function occasionally take place. New operations emerge quite suddenly, demanding a heavy investment of institutional resources for which no long-range projections or plans can be found. How does this happen?

When an organization operates out of an extrapolation/projection model of planning, extrapolations and planning presuppose the existing direction, resources, and goals of the organization. Because the managers and workers in a Christian organization tend to invest the concept of the will of God in the day-to-day operations and existence of the organization, a gap occurs between the organization's present and its future. As we have suggested, when the future is "planned" as a method of extrapolation, prognosis, and projection, the long-range plan tends to be ignored.

Now in many cases the fact that a plan tends to be ignored once it is completed may be due primarily to poor management. However, I suspect that there is another factor as well. If the managers and workers in a Christian organization experience the will of God as only a vague sense of the organization's role in God's overall plan, there will be a tendency to see the plan as unrealistic or irrelevant to day-to-day operations. Many managers operate on an informal list of priorities that are reviewed and revised regularly. This list ordinarily has higher visibility in the manager's life than does the long-range plan.

This gap between the planning process and the managing process can be viewed as a gap between an organization's present and its future. If planning is based on method alone, the future as God's will experienced as both promise and purpose will not be grasped. This is because no method can transfer the will of God from an organization to a plan for the future.

A visionary leader of a Christian organization who senses this gap will instinctively act for the good of the organization and its future by seeking the will of God in quite specific ways. Here again, priorities emerge that were not identified in the planning process through extrapolation and projection. Ordinarily, these would be fed into the planning process so that the plan becomes inspired by promise as well as informed by assumptions and projections. If it should happen that the planning process and leadership priorities become separated, then the long-range plan itself will have a limited value. There is always a value to the planning process. But when the plan is not clearly seen to have a strong priority as to the will of God, it will have less value and tend to become obsolete or, even worse, it will fail as a process of determining God's future for the organization.

This situation reveals the fact that there is often a good deal of ambivalence in the leading and managing of Christian organizations. The leaders of Christian organizations more and more tend to want good management of the organization, which usually means better methods, including better methods of planning and accounting. The need for better methods of management in order to survive in the marketplace of Christian organizational activity overcomes the uneasy conscience of many Christian leaders about using secular methods. However, these leaders often attempt to "baptize" the methods into the life and mission of the organization so that the methods can serve the will of God. This, of course, as we have shown, is problematical, to say the least. And this is the source of the ambivalence.

Leaders of Christian organizations often sense that more is needed than a better method. They may instinctively come to trust their own vision, if not their hunches, more than they do the planning process. Because they are responsible for continuing to think out the implications of the mission statement of the organization, they tend to think of the will of God more in terms of mission than in terms of organizational life and planning. However, this tends to make the planning process within the organization an ambivalent process, and also tends to separate the leadership and management functions of the organization.

I used the above scenario to develop the concept of moving toward the future primarily through methods of extrapolation, prognosis, and planning. I did not intend to depict such methods as unneccessary or irrelevant to sound management of organizations. Rather, I intended to demonstrate the problem that arises when the will of God is identified with method as a way of moving toward the future. It can be difficult to integrate the will of God with the planning process, and difficult to extricate the will of God from the existence of the organization itself.

We need at this point to consider the implications of complementing method as a process of planning with that of preparing the way, as depicted in Figure 6 above. In this perspective, where future is viewed as *adventus* rather than as *futurum*, the future is awaited and anticipated, rather than simply an extrapolation out of the present. Anticipation is not merely a projection of wishes and hopes into the future. Nor is it a direct equation of private dreams and hopes with the will of God. Rather, by viewing the future as promise before it becomes a wish or a hope, the future comes to us in the present as that which takes hold of our present with a view to opening it up to God's purpose and work.

Yes, this sounds abstract and vague, I know. All this talk of the future coming into the present could be sheer rhetoric, if not foolishness. However, we are trying to create a perspective different from our typical linear type of thinking and acting. When we speak of promise as well as of planning, we are on sound biblical ground. Abraham and Sarah had a plan that was designed to accomplish the will of God and bring forth the promised seed. But they resorted to extrapolation out of the present, and saw in Hagar a potential for bringing to fulfillment the promise of an heir—and thus Ishmael was born. In this case, the promise was no longer heard as the Word of God coming to Abraham, but became embedded in method. When God appeared again to Abraham thirteen years later, the promise was repeated—Sarah, despite her barrenness, was to bear the promised son. Ishmael was rejected as the future seed and, instead, the promise again had to be factored into the present situation. But this time with faith and hope. And to this present situation, with its unpromising and uncompromising barrenness, came Isaac as the realization of God's future (Gen. 15–16; 18; 21).

John the Baptist, of course, is the biblical figure who most dramatically and powerfully compels us to think in terms of "preparing the way of the Lord" (Mark 1:3). This messianic promise created an expectation that reached into the present and sought to prepare the way for the advent of the Lord. Again, what is worth noting is that the future, in this sense, does not result from an extrapolation out of the present into speculative or innovative choices, but rather forces the choice to be made within the context of the present as to what features and factors of the present can be seen to be in the process of preparing the way for the coming One as the presence and power of God.

In other words, it is not what might come to pass that we anticipate, but what will take place in our midst as the presence and power of God's kingdom. Rather than attempt to "make something out of the future" through method or technique, we seek to understand and make manifest what God is making out of our present as a preparation for the kingdom.

It is also noteworthy that the biblical concept of revelation is not a form of "seeing into the future" but rather that of the "breaking into the present" on the part of the future. The Greek word *apocalypse* is the word we translate as "revelation." Thus, the book of Revelation is called in the Greek "The Apocalypse." Its focus is not on speculation about the future, but upon that which is coming into the present time and place. True, the book has implications for our future existence, for we are told that "he will wipe away every tear from their eyes, and death shall be no more" (21:4). However, this is preceded by the promise that the new Jerusalem is "coming down out of heaven" (21:2), and God "will dwell with them, and they shall be his people" (21:3).

What does this mean for us? How does "preparing the way" resolve the ambivalence we spoke of earlier? Specifically, how does the task of managing Christian organizations relate to the will of God in terms of preparing the way?

As we focus on these questions, we need to be reminded again that "preparing the way," as a process of discerning

God's will, does not mean a neglect of the analytical task of
forecasting and planning based on resources, needs, and the
mission mandate of the organization—extrapolation may be a
valuable tool in planning. Nor does it mean that one should
despise past tradition or the present age in favor of a new
order that is coming. One could read the story of John the
Baptist as a rejection of such continuity and projection. His
cry, "The axe is laid to the root of the tree" (Matt. 3:10),
appears to give license to devastate or destroy the present in
hopes that the new would appear as a necessary result of such
repudiation. However, to read it this way would be to fall back
upon method again, with an overinvestment in the so-called
prophetic task of bringing in the kingdom of God through
denouncing this age in the desperate hope of bringing in the
new.

Besides, this would be a misreading of the mission and message of John. He saw quite clearly that his true task was not to
denounce but to announce. His task was not to bring in the
future through denouncing the present, but to announce the
presence of the One who would enter into the present and
bring with him the power and glory of God. The way of the
Lord, as John clearly saw, was not a way from the present into
the future, but the way of the kingdom of God into the present. What is even more interesting is that this "way of the
Lord" would emerge out of John's present activity of preaching and baptizing. John did not seek to prepare for the kingdom of God by merely projecting into the future, but by
looking closely at his present mission and activity for signs that
the coming One was even now making an appearance.

The preparing of the way is not the creating of that which is
radically new, nor is it itself an innovation that moves mission
into fulfillment. Rather, preparing of the way is an act of
"giving way" to fulfillment as it comes into view in the midst of
our present activity and mission. "I am not the bridegroom,"
said John, but the "friend of the bridegroom," the one who
"rejoices greatly at the bridegroom's voice." And then he added his own epilogue, "He must increase, but I must decrease"
(John 3:29-30).

Well and good, some might say. But how does this relate to
the hiring of a new field director when we are already running
a budget deficit for the current fiscal year? Is the new field

director the will of God for our organization, or is it a balanced financial report to the board of trustees at the end of the year? You have preached a nice chapel message for our staff, but now the administrative team had better go into executive session because it has some hard decisions to make!

How can we apply our discussion about the will of God and preparing of the way to this situation? First, we need to recognize, as we suggested earlier, that there is a fundamental ambivalence concerning the will of God in Christian organizations whenever the will of God is identified with the existence of the organization itself. (Such ambivalence is reflected in the protest in the preceding paragraph.) The mission statement of the organization (assuming that there is one!) is probably buried in the files along with the corporate documents. The trustees received an annual plan document at the beginning of the year, which gave priorities to objectives and keyed them to funding sources, and correlated it all with the projected budget. When the annual plan is consulted, it is discovered that the new field director's salary is not in the budget; but even more troublesome is the discovery that this position is not in the long-range plan. In fact, when the plan was formalized there wasn't even a "field" for which a director was needed!

What happened? Well, in our hypothetical scenario, the president of the organization was contacted early in the year by church representatives from an area not otherwise serviced by the organization. Following a tour of the area, the president heard a "Macedonian call" and deployed some field staff personnel to assist the churches in developing a relief project for impoverished peasants. Discretionary funds within the existing budget permitted short-range commitments to this project, which was already in place!

Here is the point at which the ambivalence emerges. Because the mission statement underlies the existence of the organization, and because the long-range plan, buttressed with sound principles of management by objectives and budget projections, is taken to uphold the will of God for the organization, the "Macedonian call," along with the "hunch" of the president and coupled with the availability of "discretionary funds" creates a problem.

There is a double bind here. Effective leadership and sound

management depend upon room and resources for discretionary decisions and actions. A plan and a budget should not be a straitjacket but rather a set of goals and guidelines for responsible action. However, if leaders perceive the will of God as a license for seizing opportunities and setting priorities as they occur, there may be uncertainty and confusion in the use of the plan. The organization will be caught in the bind between a systems approach to planning and discretionary leadership. The result is ambivalence concerning the will of God.

The degree of ambivalence an organization experiences in determining the will of God will be directly related to the amount of discretionary leadership in the organization and discretionary resources to back up that leadership. The more an organization tends to project its own mission and objectives through management principles the more ambivalence it will experience with its leadership.

In the early years of a strongly entrepreneurial Christian organization, this ambivalence is usually very low because the mission of the organization is heavily invested in the leader. The management functions of the organization at that time also tend to have a low visibility in the decision-making process. As the organization matures it tends to resort to better principles of management, because organizations tend to become more systematic and to create their own management needs and also because the organization will need to become efficient in order to survive.

What is often not realized in such a transition is that the will of God, which originally was strongly invested in leadership and mission, becomes increasingly identified with the existence of the organization itself and thus becomes extended into the methods by which the organization is managed. Responsible managers of Christian organizations tend to resist unplanned and unbudgeted innovation, but also feel uneasy over the rejection of "Macedonian calls," particularly when the discussion turns to the "will of God." Strong commitment to organizational management tends to produce conservative styles of Christian organizations, unless that commitment to management can be creatively tied to a concept of "preparing the way."

Preparing the way, as a style of managing Christian organizations, turns ambivalence into creative tension. There is no avoiding the tension between the present age and the kingdom of God that is coming into the present. This was made clear in the preceding chapter. Now we can begin to see the relevance of that tension. The problem with ambivalence is that it is destructive to the creative relation between imagination and planning. Ambivalence fears promise as much as it distrusts planning. Where the will of God is caught in ambivalence, it either tends to be capricious (if there are discretionary funds available!) or cowardly. The thrust of our argument is that promises and plans are creatively related and can and ought to work together.

When preparing the way becomes the style of management for Christian organizations, discernment is linked with discretion in such a way that the planning process begins with an evaluation of the present in terms of containing a sign of what is to come. The will of God is neither identified with "hunches" nor with projections of the past into the future. The will of God is that which must be discerned in the creative tension between what is and what is to come. Thus, managers of Christian organizations must be as competent in discerning promises as in directing planning. But this is what is distinctive about a Christian organization itself! And this is what is distinctive about managing Christian organizations.

Discerning the promise of God calls for reflection upon the mission of an organization from biblical and theological perspectives. This ongoing task is central to the task of management, though not exclusively the task of management. Such reflection begins at the point of recruiting and hiring staff who work in Christian organizations. Those who work within Christian organizations as well as those who manage Christian organizations (including trustees or directors) should be encouraged to believe in and seek what is promised by God to the organization. Everyone who is part of a Christian organization ought to have a stake in the promise as well as in the program. But the promise cannot become merely the theme of the chapel services; it must also be the substance of the present activity and the source of management wisdom.

This creative, ongoing task of relating promise to projections will keep Christian organizations open to the will of God at each phase of the administrative and decision-making process. Discretionary leadership can be seen as an investment of the organization in its own mission statement. As such, it should not be detached from the ongoing task of management, nor should it be detached from the system of budget planning and control. The strategic planning process of a Christian organization is actually a discretionary process. When all of the cost accounting history has been tabulated, when all of the organizational objectives have been listed and given priorities, when all of the trends have been analyzed and evaluated, that is the point to exercise the discretionary wisdom of preparing the way. Here is where promise needs to be factored in and the will of God invested in persons, not merely in plans. And when this takes place, strategic planning comes alive and is a relevant and creative process.

The will of God is not bound up in decisions but in decision makers. In the same way, the will of God is bound up in the mission of an organization, not in the organization itself. Whenever the will of God becomes identical with the existence of an organization, of a plan, or of a decision, it yields itself to method, and not to preparation of the way. Methods, which involve organizational forms and strategies, management principles, and strategic planning, all can be brought into preparation of the way. It may even be that the promise emerges through the process of using some method, but it always stands in a creative tension with method, and thus links us with the will of God.

It comes down to this. The will of God links a Christian organization with the mission of God in the world through the particular mission statement of the organization. The formation of a mission statement involves the Christian organization in the creative task of discerning the will of God in terms of specific objectives and functions that will be determinative of that organization's life and purpose. In creating the mission statement, the Christian organization responds to the vision and leadership of persons who carry a heavy investment of the organization's discernment of the will of God in terms of trust and commitment directed toward the leaders. The leaders of Christian organizations respond to the mission statement by directing the life and resources of the organization in such a way that members of the organization each experience to some degree a sense of accomplishing the will of God through the mission and work of God in the world. The day-to-day operations of managing the organization, as well as the long-range strategies and plans of the organization, remain open both to the promise of God as articulated in the mission statement and to the unexpected needs and opportunities that arise to challenge the organization's set plan.

To return to our scenario, it should be determined whether or not the field director is a "candidate for baptism" long before the budget crisis! Or, to put it another way, the executive "hunch" should be made part of the executive "lunch" at which the will of God is discussed.

Can persons be prepared to give such leadership to Christian organizations? Can leaders be prepared to lead in "preparing the way"? Of course they can, and it will be the further purpose of this book to show how they can.

CHAPTER FOUR

LEADERSHIP DEVELOPMENT FOR CHRISTIAN ORGANIZATIONS

"Any player can catch a ball," a manager of a professional baseball team once said, "but you do not become a catcher on my team until you demonstrate leadership—and the players will be the judge of that."

In baseball, the catcher, not the pitcher, calls the signals. This is quite different from football, where the one who throws the ball also calls the signals. Without pressing this analogy too far, one might dare to suggest that managing a Christian organization is more like being a catcher on a baseball team than being the quarterback on a football team.

A catcher, of course, does more than simply catch whatever ball is pitched. He must call for the right pitch in the right situation, but all within the capabilities of the pitcher to throw it. This is why the manager cited above expected his catcher to demonstrate competence in leadership. The catcher, in effect, must read the situation correctly, direct the pitcher to use his talent most effectively, and yes, learn to keep his eyes open when the batter swings at the ball! And even though catchers do not have a "win/loss" record as do pitchers, the first person a pitcher ordinarily thanks after winning a game is his catcher.

So it is with managers of Christian organizations. The ball is in somebody else's hand, and yet the signals that put the ball into play and mobilize every member of the team into action come from behind the plate. This is why the one who runs the team from the dugout is called the manager, while the player on the field who enables the talents of others to rise to their best is called a leader. It might be interesting to reflect upon this with regard to the place of leadership in managing Christian organizations.

We have seen that the nature and purpose of Christian organizations are to interpret and implement the will of God as revealed through Jesus Christ, so that God is glorified and his own creative and redemptive purpose realized. The managing of Christian organizations is not done effectively from the dugout, to take the baseball analogy one step further. Nor is the manager like a quarterback in a football game where the coach sends all the plays in from the bench. The manager of the Christian organization is "on the field of play," so to speak, and the game is called from behind the plate.

For this reason, we prefer not to separate the concept and role of leader and manager. Christian organizations, like all organizations, must be managed. But those responsible for managing the organization must also be effective in leadership. Therefore, the development of leadership for Christian organizations will be the central theme for the remainder of this book.

It may be surprising to some, but there is no biblical model for a leader as we ordinarily use the word. That is, there is no model for a person who occupies the office or position of leader whose authority is vested in him by virtue of the office. Even Jesus did not present himself as a leader by virtue of his position. Rather, he referred to himself as a shepherd and said that he did not come to be served, but to serve (John 10:11; Matt. 20:28). He accepted the designation of Messiah, but deferred in all matters to the One who sent him. While he is called an apostle and high priest, he is recognized as having only the authority that is delegated to him by the Father (Heb. 3:1-2).

In fact, Jesus contrasted the way in which the "rulers of the Gentiles" exercise the role of a leader through vested authority and power with the way in which his own disciples were to exercise leadership as servants (Matt. 20:25-28) These Gentile "rulers" exemplified the "leader/follower" model, in which the leader is vested with authority as well as with the power to carry out his commands. Those who were to provide leadership in the kingdom of God, by contrast, were to be followers and servants of God as Jesus himself was.

The role of the leader as the Gentiles practiced it carried with it an assumption concerning the use of power to achieve the wishes of the leader. What is wrong with this model of the leader is that it tends to equate authority with power. Jesus, on the other hand, spoke as one having authority (Mark 1:11; 2:10) but not ultimate power. Power belongs to God in heaven, and Jesus will sit on the "right hand of power" in the eschaton (Luke 22:69).

Even the authority Jesus has is from God, who is the original "author" from whom all authority comes. "There is no authority except from God" (Rom. 13:1). All authority is given to Jesus (Matt. 28:18), but he bears this authority as the Son of the Father, not by virtue of an office or position. It was his obedience as the Son that lay behind his exercise of authority; thus, the power to which his authority pointed resided ultimately in God the Father, who had sent him.

Dietrich Bonhoeffer, in a powerful and perceptive essay entitled "The Concept of the Leader," has pointed out the dangers inherent in seeing the role of leader as the Gentiles saw it in Jesus' day. In this essay, first delivered over the German radio on February 1, 1933, Bonhoeffer criticized the then current "Leadership Principle"—*das Führerprinzip,* as Hitler called it. The concept of the leader, Bonhoeffer said, has produced the specter of an independent figure.

> In the case of the Leader, the essential thing is the supremacy of his person. In both cases a power-relationship is involved; in leadership the important thing is the superiority of something neutral and objective, in the case of the Leader it is the superiority of his person. . . . It is virtually impossible to give a rational basis for the nature of the Leader . . . the focus of leadership is the person being led, the line of vision goes from above downwards, while the focus of the Leader is the Leader himself and the line of vision goes from below upwards.[1]

Thus, we prefer not to speak of a "leader" but rather of *leadership* as a distinctive quality and responsibility of those

---

1. D. Bonhoeffer, *No Rusty Swords* (New York: Harper and Row, 1965), pp. 188ff. Not surprisingly, the newly appointed minister of propaganda cut this prepared address off the air before it could be completed. Only two days earlier, Hitler had been installed as Reich Chancellor of Germany.

who manage Christian organizations. In this and the next two chapters we will examine the following three specific aspects of leadership and relate them to the managing of Christian organizations:

1. Effective leadership means reading the signs of God's promise in the context of present events, and translating these signs into goals; this is "preparing the way of the Lord."

2. Effective leadership means directing and coordinating the energies and resources of the organization toward realization of the goals; this is being a "faithful steward" of God's business.

3. Effective leadership means maintaining quality control over the character and purpose of the organization; this is to "give proof before the churches" of love and obedience to Christ (2 Cor. 8:24).

Our purpose in this chapter, then, is to explore the first aspect of leadership: reading the signs of God's promise in the context of present events, and translating these signs into goals. Our goal is to define leadership as a function of managing Christian organizations in such a way that it becomes clear what "preparing the way of the Lord" means in terms of enabling a Christian organization to define its goals in light of its mission. Our thesis in this chapter is that leadership is a gift God desires to give to managers of Christian organizations, and that managers can develop this gift as they learn how to "call the game from behind the plate," to return to our baseball metaphor.

In the previous chapter, we concluded our discussion of the distinction between "preparation of the way" and "method" by saying that one must bring the promise of God into the planning process, and not merely extrapolate out of the present into the future. We cited the case of John the Baptizer, who announced the appearance of the Messiah by pointing to the signs that were even then apparent in their midst. The "way of the Lord" that John proclaimed was indeed the advent of the future into the present, and he called for "giving way" to the fulfillment of this promise by receiving the gift through repentance, faith, and obedience. Pointing beyond himself and his own ministry, John exercised his leadership by singling

out Jesus as the Lord and retreating, himself, into the background.

This aspect of leadership—reading the signs of God's
promise—is a gift that managers of Christian organizations
can—and must—develop. Those who have been noted for
exceptional leadership in managing Christian organizations
have often been called people of unusual vision. These persons apparently saw something that others did not, and,
moved by that vision, were unusually successful in persuading
others to take up the vision and transform it into a project or
task—and, in some cases, into an organization with international scope and influence.

It would be a mistake, however, to assume that this gift is
some kind of clairvoyance by which one is privileged to see into
the future. The gift by which one reads the signs of God's
promise is not that at all. If it were, it would belong more to the
realm of the occult than to God's work of reconciliation. In our
discussion of leadership development we must first identify
this gift of vision.

THE VISION OF LEADERSHIP

The vision of leadership, we must say first of all, is from above
to below, from the future to the present—not from the present
to the future. The one who sees the signs of God's promise is
first of all a student of the promises! Through meditation
upon the work of God in the history of salvation as depicted by
the inspired authors of the Old Testament, John the Baptizer
looked at his contemporary world through the lens of divine
revelation, rooted in divine action. Rather than peer into the
future, John looked piercingly at the present and sought to
interpret the events taking place around him in light of the
promises of God.

It is quite likely that John began his ministry of summoning
his contemporaries to a baptism of repentance based upon the
all-too-obvious signs that theirs was an evil generation. By
reading these signs in terms of God's judgment and promise,
and by investing in his own ministry the authority of God's
Word, he thereby attracted the promised one to himself. John
did not need to go out and hunt for the Messiah; rather, Jesus

came to him. We search the Scripture record in vain for the clues by which John recognized that his cousin, Jesus of Nazareth, was indeed the "one who is to come." But recognize him he did, and, in the context of his own ministry, pointed him out as the one who would create the new order and bring in the new covenant.

The vision that belongs to leadership is not an esoteric quality only certain mystics have. Rather, it is a gift one can develop through meditation on God's revealed Word and serious attention to the human situation and the historical present. What accounts for the unusual perception and creative leadership offered by the theologian Karl Barth at the very time that the wave of nineteenth-century German liberal theology was cresting and crashing? Those who knew him said that he was a man who studied with equal seriousness the Bible in one hand and the daily newspaper in the other.

"A mark of leaders, an attribute that puts them in a position to show the way for others," writes Robert Greenleaf, "is that they are better than most at pointing the direction."[2] But this requires an aptitude for reading the signs as well as translating them into specific goals. This aptitude can be cultivated through a creative process of reflection upon what has been promised combined with a serious commitment to a ministry based upon what is an obvious need. The promise, and the vision, comes to the one who is intelligently and expectantly at work.

It is no doubt true, though seldom recognized, that those who have demonstrated unusual gifts of leadership in developing Christian organizations have also acquired a keen intelligence about the nature and meaning of God's Word. I do not see that the development of leadership as an aspect of managing Christian organizations can take place without acquiring the gift of discernment with regard to the signs of God's promise in present events. The Bible is much more than a devotional handbook for managers of Christian organizations. It is a casebook of promises that are meant to inform anyone who takes seriously the present events as creating the new agenda for the mission of God's redemptive work in this world.

Does this mean that managers of Christian organizations

2. R. Greenleaf, *Servant Leadership* (New York: Paulist Press, 1977).

need to undergo training as theologians and biblical scholars? Of course not—at least not in the formal and academic sense. It must also be said, however, that managers of Christian organizations who wish to develop leadership gifts in the area of discerning the signs of God's promises can hardly afford to neglect serious meditation and study of the Bible as a casebook of God's promises. An academic degree in biblical studies can be a helpful way to prepare for such use of the Bible in leadership management. Yet many who become managers of Christian organizations no longer have the opportunity for such formal academic preparation. However, many Bible colleges and seminaries offer continuing education programs in biblical studies—at both credit and noncredit levels—to those already involved in management of Christian organizations.

One would miss the thrust of what is being presented here, however, if it was assumed that formal study of the Bible will in every case result in the gift of leadership. If this were true, theological seminaries would be turning out graduates with certified competence in leadership! No, the development of a leadership that enables one to recognize the signs of the promise of God and to translate these signs into goals for the people of God does not come with a diploma or a certificate. Such leadership is a gift that is acquired, not a procedure that can be taught. It is acquired through the chemistry that is produced when one combines biblical literacy with a compelling conviction that God is at work through one's own life as offered up in service to Christ. It is produced though the on-going dialogue between the Word of God and the desperate needs of human society. It is discovered through the humbling exercise of retracing one's steps in order to get back to the strategic center. The apostle Paul, for example, did not receive the vision that pointed to Macedonia until after turning back from two unsuccessful endeavors to push on into northern Asia Minor (Acts 16:6-10).

"Never trust a person who has never made a mistake," my father once told me. I suspect that those who followed Paul's leadership in crossing over into Macedonia were convinced more by what they sensed Paul learned by being guided by the Spirit, and by his own willingness to change directions, than they were by his enthusiasm about a dream during the night. Sometimes the most effective leadership is marked by the sense to change directions when it is clear that a mistake has been made.

When the catcher walks out to the pitcher's mound after the batter has just hit a home run, it is usually not to berate the pitcher for throwing a bad pitch, but to acknowledge that it was the wrong call on his part. One gains the clues that enable a catcher to call a good game during the World Series through the home runs hit in July.

So, too, leadership is an art that one can develop, and vision is a gift that one can acquire—but only through the chemistry that occurs when promise is mixed with practice. The vision of leadership, we have said, is from above to below, from the future to the present, from promise to practice.

THE PURPOSE OF LEADERSHIP

The purpose of leadership, we now want to say, is to build community, not merely to perform tasks. That is, leadership from a biblical perspective is not so much task oriented as it is community oriented, although in many cases it does involve the performance of a task or the enabling and equipping of others to perform tasks. Moses was given the task of leading the children of Israel out of slavery in Egypt into the freedom and blessedness of the promised land. But in studying the record of his leadership as recorded in Exodus, Leviticus, Numbers, and Deuteronomy, it becomes quite clear that the purpose of his leadership was the establishing of a community that embodied the Word of God through every aspect of its social, civil, economic, and religious life.

Moses read God's promise not only in terms of the most expeditious method of moving a horde of people from one geographical location to another, but of developing a loosely knit conglomeration of tribal families into a "people of God." Thus, he ascended Mt. Sinai not to receive a strategic plan for moving the people across the wilderness into the promised land, but to receive the law of God and to translate the promise into specific goals for the formation of a community that would embody the character of God himself (see Exod. 19–40).

Only a few months after leaving Egypt, the people were

poised on the very borders of the land of promise. For all practical purposes, their goal was at hand, in terms of actually entering into the land. At this point, however, there was a lack of faith on the part of the majority of the scouts sent in to spy out the land, and the people "murmured against Moses" and turned their hearts and their backs on the promise and determined to go back again to Egypt (Num. 13:25–14:10). It was quite clear to Moses that the people themselves were not prepared to enter into the land. The primary task of developing them into an obedient and faithful community had not yet been completed.

What is remarkable about the leadership of Moses is not that he took the shortest route to the promise as a task to be completed, but that he correctly read the promise in terms of building a community of people, and then spent forty years with them wandering through the wilderness. In the end, he succeeded in holding them together as a people with whom God had covenanted, even through their continued disobedience and unfaithfulness, and brought them again to the borders of the promised land.

In the end, Moses surrendered leadership to Joshua, who did finally lead the people into the land of promise. Why Joshua? Because he had shown almost forty years earlier that he had the vision from above to below, from the promise to the practice. It was Joshua and Caleb, those two alone, who brought back a "good report" of the land when sent in to spy it out, who pleaded with the people to go up and possess the land, saying, "If the Lord delights in us, he will bring us into this land" (Num. 14:6-8).

The purpose of leadership, we are saying, is primarily to develop a community of people, not merely to complete a task. This distinctive qualifies the concept of leadership from a biblical perspective. The mark of Christian leadership is set in this purpose. God's essential and primary task, if we may put it that way, is to create a people who reflect his own character and who exist for his glory and praise. All other tasks that occupy human persons and demand the investment of human will and energies are qualified by this divine task.

When we look at Jesus himself, we see a person who does not let tasks blind him to the purpose for which he is sent. He, too, exercises leadership by calling the twelve to follow him. In the end, however, he recognizes that the purpose of his leadership is not to be completed merely by a headlong rush to die upon a cross, but by developing in his disciples a sense of community in his own body and blood.

As we read the gospel narratives of his life and approaching death, we see that Jesus turns aside from every opportunity to bring about the kingdom of God through tasks of healing and other miracles. He deliberately shuns positions that would offer him power and recognition as a "leader." Instead, he turns more and more to the twelve disciples that the Father has given to him. And in the end, in his high priestly prayer, he gives account to the Father for those who had been given him, certifying that he has indeed developed in them a true knowledge of God and that his joy is fulfilled in them (John 17:1-19).

For his part, the apostle Paul interprets his mission in terms of establishing communities of Christian believers, exercising his leadership first and foremost in the nurture and care of these communities. While others have letters or credentials certifying their authority as apostles and leaders, Paul considers this unnecessary, writing to the Corinthian Christians: "Do we need, as some do, letters of recommendation to you, or from you? You yourselves are our letter of recommendation, . . . written not with ink but with the Spirit of the living God, not on tablets of stone but on tablets of human hearts" (2 Cor. 3:1-3). And to the Christian community at Thessalonica he writes: "For what is our hope or joy or crown of boasting before our Lord Jesus at his coming? Is it not you? For you are our glory and joy" (1 Thess. 2:19-20).

Paul reveals to us many insights into the nature of leadership from a Christian perspective. Foremost is the way in which he is able to relate goals to purpose with respect to mission. We have said that a critical aspect of leadership is the gift of being able to read the signs of promise and translate them into specific goals. Many people appear to be able to translate vision into goals, but this is not yet leadership from a Christian perspective. What Paul reveals to us is that subtle but critical link between goals that translate vision and purpose that determines the priorities for leadership.

Paul had a clear vision that the gospel must be brought to all of his known world. He translated this vision into a specific goal of going to Spain via the church at Rome. The very fact that he included Rome in his itinerary reveals to us his recognition that the building of community was essential to the purpose of God. Thus he writes a letter to the Christians at Rome so that they may be strengthened and encouraged by him (1:11), but also that he may be strengthened and encouraged by them (1:12).

Yet there is a more immediate priority for Paul, which delays his plan to go to Spain: his intention to take a gift for the poor among the Christians in Jerusalem, which has been raised from the churches in Asia, Macedonia, and Greece. The journey to Spain will not occur at the expense of a ministry to build up the community of Christians at Jerusalem. Paul's apostolic leadership always contained specific goals as the translation of promise into a plan of action. He did not, however, invest his leadership solely in the achieving of a goal or a plan. He recognized very clearly that the purpose of leadership is directed toward the building of community, not merely the completion of a task.

Clearly, there is a tension here between the goals that produce action plans and the purpose of building community through which the goals are to be reached. The mark of Christian leadership comes precisely at this point. Christian leadership is a form of competence in managing the priorities that relate goals to purpose. Those who learn to recognize and manage priorities in this creative tension bring leadership into the task of management.

THE GIFTEDNESS OF LEADERSHIP

The New Testament makes it quite clear that the leadership of the church is a gifted leadership. We have argued in the early part of this book that Christian organizations are paraparochial forms of the church. As such, they exist alongside of and beyond the geographical limitations of the local parish church and also are recipients of the gifts Christ gives to his church (Eph. 4:7-14). Are those who exercise leadership of these paraparochial Christian organizations gifted in the same sense as those who exercise pastoral leadership in the local church? The answer is Yes. Because of this we say that involved in the development of leadership for Christian organizations is the development of spiritual gifts as appropriate to the leadership task.

I do not intend to develop here the biblical basis for the role of spiritual gifts in the church. That has been done competently and thoroughly by others.[3] The assumption that I am making in this discussion is that the biblical term "spiritual gifts," as a translation of the Greek *charismata* (1 Cor. 12:1), is a special gift bestowed upon individuals by the Holy Spirit for the purpose of effecting the ministry of Christ in and through the church, which includes Christian organizations.

In an essay entitled "The Continuing Charismatic Structure," Hans Küng lists several aspects of the *charismata,* or spiritual gifts, that underlie the approach being taken here:[4]

1. The spiritual gifts are everyday phenomena, not exceptional. The purposes of the spiritual gifts are to exalt Jesus as Lord (1 Cor. 12:1-2; 1 John 4:2-3) and to result in service for and through the community of Christ (1 Cor. 12:7).

2. The spiritual gifts are diverse rather than uniform in nature and function. What is noteworthy concerning Paul's reference to the gifts is their diversity; there is no apparent number making it a "closed list." Representative lists are given in 1 Cor. 12:28-31; Rom. 12:6-8; Eph. 4:11.

3. The spiritual gifts are for the many rather than for the few. Not only are they everyday gifts rather than occasional, and not only are they various in function rather than limited; they are also widely distributed among the members of the church rather than restricted to a hierarchical few. Each Christian is "charismatic," having been given the *charism* of eternal life as a gift (Rom. 6:23). So also each has a special gift from God, one of one kind and one of another (1 Cor. 7:7).

4. The spiritual gifts are a continuing phenomenon in the church, not restricted to the first century. Not only are there no indications that the gifts were originally designed to serve

3. Some recent helpful contributions in this area include Howard Carter. *Spiritual Gifts and their Operation* (Springfield: Gospel Publishing House, 1968); Kenneth C. Kinghorn, *Gifts of the Spirit* (Nashville: Abingdon Press, 1976); C. Peter Wagner, *Your Spiritual Gifts Can Help Your Church Grow* (Glendale, Calif.: Regal Books, 1979); and Elmer L. Towns, "An Analysis of the Gift of Faith in Church Growth," D.Min. diss. Fuller Theological Seminary, 1983.
4. H. Küng, *The Church* (London: Sheed and Ward, 1967).

only during the early formulation of the church, but there are explicit promises in Scripture that the Spirit would continue to give gifts to the members of the church for the work of the ministry. Paul teaches that there is one Spirit, not two, with one function at one time and another function at another. So, too, he says that Jesus has given gifts to his church for the work of the ministry "until we all attain to the unity of the faith and of the knowledge of the Son of God, to mature manhood, to the measure of the stature of the fulness of Christ" (Eph. 4:13). Clearly, the church has not yet achieved this goal.

Küng further defines a spiritual gift as "the call of God, addressed to an individual, to a particular ministry in the community, which brings with it the ability to fulfill that ministry."[5]

Thus, it is proper to speak of the giftedness of leadership for Christian organizations. Those who exercise leadership should seek to identify spiritual gifts that are appropriate for their own special tasks, while the organization should confirm them in their exercise of these gifts.

In our discussion, then, we will only suggest how several spiritual gifts can relate to the leadership of Christian organizations. Our list is not exclusive; nor are these gifts the most important or strategic.

First, leadership may have the *gift of exhortation,* which we might call the ability to enable others to care. Paul writes to the church in Rome, "Having gifts . . . let us use them: . . . he who exhorts, in his exhortation" (12:6, 8). Certainly one who exercises leadership will need the ability to motivate others to seek the same vision and to care about the same project, which leads to the goal.

When Paul wrote to the Corinthians, hoping to motivate them to participate in the project to raise support for the needy Christians in Jerusalem, he wrote from a position of leadership in a paraparochial organization. This was not a project of any local church, nor did Paul make use of apostolic authority to command and extort a gift. He relied, instead, upon his gift of exhortation, upon persuasion. "You are not restricted by us, but you are restricted in your own affections,"

5. Ibid, p. 256.

he wrote. "In return—I speak as to children—widen your hearts also" (2 Cor. 6:12-13). This is the gift of exhortation— enabling others *to care.*

Second, leadership may well seek the *gift of faith,* which is the ability to enable others to act. This was one of the gifts Paul encouraged the Corinthians to seek (1 Cor. 12:9). Clearly, it is not saving faith, for that is given to all who are given the gift of salvation in Christ (Eph. 2:8). The gift of faith is a special endowment of leadership that moves caring into action.[6]

It is one thing to motivate others to care; it is another to motivate them into action. Jesus related faith to action quite specifically. "Have faith in God," he said. "Whoever says to this mountain, Be taken up and cast into the sea,' and does not doubt in his heart, but believes that what he says will come to pass, it will be done for him" (Mark 11:22-23).

Paul certainly felt that he had motivated the Corinthian Christians to care about the benevolence project, but he also knew that he had to motivate them into action. He did this by citing the example of the faith of the Macedonians, who had already made their contribution. Now Paul writes to the Corinthians, urging them to "excel in this gracious work also" (2 Cor. 8:7). This is the gift of faith—enabling others *to act.*

A third spiritual gift that is appropriate to the leadership of Christian organizations is the *gift of administration,* or enabling others to organize. In his first letter to the Corinthian Christians, Paul reminds them of this gift (1 Cor. 12:28). In his second letter we see this gift in operation, as Paul gives leadership to the project of raising support for the poor in the church at Jerusalem. There is an obvious administrative task connected with this gift. People in various parts of the world need to be organized in order for the project to succeed.

In this same letter Paul reveals how Titus puts the various gifts of leadership to use:

> Thanks be to God who puts the same earnest care for you into the heart of Titus. For he not only accepted our appeal [the gift of exhortation], but . . . he is going to you of his own accord [the gift of faith]. With him we are sending the brother who . . . has

---

6. For a fine exposition of the gift of faith as a gift of leadership, see Elmer Towns, "An Analysis of the Gift of Faith in Church Growth."

been appointed by the churches [the gift of administration].
(2 Cor. 8:16-19)

Paul's leadership in the fund-raising project led to a remarkable effort in motivating the churches to organize their own
activities and to appoint representatives who could accompany
the gift to Jerusalem. In this way, Paul enabled them to invest
their caring in an action in which they continued to be involved. This is obviously the secret of effective organization.
When people can invest their own concern and their own actions in the organization, it is most effective. This is the gift of
administration, enabling others *to organize*.

A fourth gift we might suggest is the *gift of stewardship*, enabling others to execute. Execution, in this sense, is the ability to
follow through with an action to successful completion, and to
be able to give a good report.

Paul mentions in his letter to the Ephesian church that the
gifts of Christ are given to the church "to equip the saints for
the work of the ministry" (4:12). To Titus he writes: "A bishop
as God's steward must . . ."; he then proceeds to list specific
qualifications and duties. A bishop is an overseer *(episcopos)* in
the church, whose responsibilities include leadership and the
gift of stewardship. In biblical times, the steward was the one
left in charge of the household and estate during the absence
of the owner. Thus, the steward is the executive who sees that
the work is executed competently—that is, according to the
will of the master of the house.

This gift of stewardship involves accountability for the *use*
of resources, not merely making resources available. Stewardship is the gift of enabling others to execute responsibility
in such a way that resources are invested wisely and effectively.
Stewardship is that which makes caring, acting, and organiz-
ing a competent execution of the will of God. Without the gift
of stewardship, leadership will tend toward exploitation and
self-service. It is, of course, the gift of stewardship that underlies what we call servant leadership. The gift of stewardship is
the gift of enabling others *to execute*.

How do those responsible for leadership in Christian organizations become "gifted" in the sense that we have suggested
above? First, by developing one's own Christian life and seek-

ing from God the gifts that are appropriate to the leadership task to which God has called him or her. Being gifted is essentially a Christian privilege, and only secondarily an asset to leadership. Second, leaders can receive gifts appropriate to their calling through involvement in Christian community, where gifts are confirmed and where the Spirit of God graciously works. While the gifts are given to individuals, they are not individual gifts. The gifts are given for the purpose of serving the ministry of Christ and for building up his body. Through the ministry of the body of Christ, which reaches into the life of Christian organizations, those who work in Christian organizations are also gifted. Leadership development is also the development of a gifted leadership.

THE CHARACTER OF LEADERSHIP

We have discussed the vision, the purpose, and the giftedness of leadership. There is a fourth dimension to leadership from a Christian perspective that we must now make more explicit. The character of leadership is related to the destiny of the people being led.

What I mean by speaking of the character of leadership is the moral aspect of leadership. That is, from a Christian perspective there is a true leadership as opposed to a false leadership. In the Old Testament, the distinction between the true and the false prophet was not merely a moral distinction based on ethical criteria. It was, rather, a distinction between those prophets who spoke truly of God's intention and purpose, and those who spoke falsely. The "lying prophet" spoke words that were congenial to the wishes of the people and their leaders, but with drastic consequences for the people. The true prophet of God often spoke words of judgment, but always as an interpretation of the promise of God, with the end result being renewal and restoration of the people for the sake of the covenant.

In our day, the leadership of Jim Jones, who led almost a thousand people to a suicidal destiny in Jonestown, is a shocking witness to the danger of a leadership that becomes detached from spiritual and moral truth. No one could dispute the effectiveness of Jones as a leader. Whatever the source of his vision, he effectively translated that vision into a spectacular goal, and even succeeded in building a community of followers. It was only in the grotesque end of that venture that its diabolical character became self-evident.

There is a warning here for us. Leadership is not self-authenticating in terms of its pragmatic and persuasive success. The nature of Christian leadership is rooted firmly in the character and purpose of God. And the character of leadership is related to the destiny of the people being led.

For Moses, the most efficient and most effective action would have been to turn the dissatisfaction of the people into a triumphant return to Egypt, where at least they had food that satisfied their craving! The character of his leadership is revealed only in the end, however, when the people are finally poised at the threshold of the promised land. For their destiny was freedom, not slavery. Their truth and their good was to be found in their conformity to God's law, not in their right to set their own destiny.

But does this mean that the character of leadership is always revealed only at the end, when it is too late? Were there no clues by which one could have recognized that the leadership of Jim Jones was destructive and leading to the doom of his followers rather than to their freedom and salvation? Of course there were. And these clues had become sufficient for many to dissociate themselves from his movement, and for some to undertake official investigation into what appeared to have become a destructive and tyrannical leadership.

Dietrich Bonhoeffer pointed perceptively to the character of community as the clue to the character of leadership:

Where there is community there is leadership . . . the group is the womb of the Leader. It gives him everything, even his authority. . . . It sees him, not in his reality but in his vocation. It is essential for the image of the Leader that the group does not see the face of the one who goes before, but sees him only from behind as the figure stepping out ahead. His humanity is veiled in his Leader's form. . . . The Leader is what no other person can be, an individual, a personality. The relationship between those led and their Leader is that the former transfer their own rights to him. It is this one form of collectivism which turns into intensified individualism. For that reason, the true concept of community, which rests on responsibility, on the recognition that individuals belong responsibly one to another finds no fulfillment here.[7]

Where leadership passes over into the concept of the Leader, Bonhoeffer rightly points to the surrender of the essence of community to the monolithic structure of the collective unit. Because the true destiny of the community as the people of God is based on covenant promise, and because that promise points to the formation of the people into a historical community, the signs of covenant promise as the true destiny of the people are evident in the quality and character of the community itself.

In much the same way one might point to the actions and attitude of a developing child and warn that the destiny of the child is already prefigured in the present character of the child's life. Parenting is a form of leadership by which children are enabled to develop into persons capable of creating and sustaining effective relationships that enhance community of persons. As with leadership, so it is with parenting; the character of the parenting process is manifest in the destiny of the children being parented.

True leadership, from a Christian perspective, must be able to preserve a deep sense of community and avoid fusing the needs and desires of the people into a collective unit, with leadership passing over into the role of the leader. The clue that this distortion is already taking place, according to Bonhoeffer, is the shift of authority from the promise by which community exists under God to the position and office of the leader. This shift brings a dehumanizing process to those who are being led, and a veiling of the true humanity of the leader. When this happens, the people no longer wish to see the face of the leader, in his human vulnerability and weakness, but only see him "from behind," as Bonhoeffer puts it, so that he becomes "larger than life," an object upon which they can project their own individualistic dreams for success and desire for power.

The one who exercizes true leadership, on the other hand, must be able to disillusion. Leadership that is authentic, and that serves the purpose of building community, said

7. D. Bonhoeffer, *No Rusty Swords*, pp. 186-200.

Bonhoeffer, must destroy the illusion that power resides in the person and office of a leader. What must and can be done, in order that leadership be preserved for the sake of community, is that the one who exercises leadership must know that he or she is deeply committed to the members of the community and most heavily laden with responsibility for sustaining this community, and, as Bonhoeffer says, must in fact "quite simply be a servant."[8]

This concept of "servant leadership," popularized by Robert Greenleaf in his book with that title, should not be misunderstood. Servant leadership does not mean a refusal to lead, nor does it mean a servile dependence upon the desires and will of the community. Greenleaf explains how he happened to come upon the concept. In reading the works of Hermann Hesse, he found in the book *Journey to the East* the story of Leo, a

> person of extraordinary presence, spirit and inspiration. Leo was actually the leader all the time, but he was servant first because that was what he was, *deep down inside*. Leadership was bestowed upon a man who was by nature a servant. It was something given, or assumed, that could be taken away.[9]

We must understand servant leadership within the context of the aspects of leadership we developed above. The vision of leadership comes from above to below, from promise to practice. Thus, servant leadership is first of all faithful service to the promise by which God's own will and intention is brought to the present. For Israel, this promise was the giving of covenant as an irrevocable commitment on the part of Yahweh to his own people. For New Testament Christian experience, the promise is the realized presence of Jesus Christ as the Messiah, who fulfills the covenant from both sides through his own obedience and faithfulness, as the divine Son. Thus, the apostle Paul continually referred to himself as the "bondslave" of Jesus Christ, and it was upon this deep inner experience and self-knowledge that he received and exercised his gift of leadership.

We saw, secondly, that the purpose of leadership is centered

8. Ibid.
9. R. Greenleaf, *Servant Leadership*, p. 7.

in the building of community, not merely in the completion of a task. Thus, servant leadership for Jesus was a responsible commitment to the divine purpose in calling a community of persons out of the world and establishing them as his own people—the body of Christ. The servant leader exists as one of those called into the community of Christ, but who also accepts the gift of responsible leadership for the sake of equipping the people of God for the task of ministry. So Paul teaches that Christ, having ascended on high, gave gifts to members of his body, "to equip the saints for the work of the ministry, for building up the body of Christ" (Eph. 4:12).

Third, we looked at the giftedness of leadership, where the Christian privilege of receiving Christ's gifts for the work of the ministry includes those who manage Christian organizations. Thus, servant leadership is essentially a gifted leadership rather than a self-serving leadership.

And then, finally, we saw that the character of leadership is related to the destiny of the people led. Thus, servant leadership is a calling and gift to exemplify the life of Christ, who gave himself for the church, his body. In his final exhortation to the elders of the church at Ephesus, Paul clearly set forth their responsibility as servant leaders: "Take heed to yourselves and to all the flock, in which the Holy Spirit has made you overseers, to care for the church of God which he obtained with the blood of his own Son" (Acts 20:28).

Our purpose in this chapter has been to define the nature of Christian leadership as an important aspect of the managing of Christian organizations. We sought to do this through an exposition of one aspect of leadership: reading the signs of promise in the context of present events and translating these signs into goals that effectively fulfill the mission of the organization.

Leadership, as we have defined it, is more than "managing from the bench," or "catching a baseball"—it is "calling the game from behind the plate." It is, in fact, "catching the vision" through exposure to God's Word and being filled with his Spirit. It is, in truth, translating the vision into a goal, or goals, and having a plan of action that captures the attention and focuses the resources and energies of others to move toward the goal. It is, in reality, first of all being a servant, and then finding a promise that can be attached to a crying need.

Leadership is the chemistry produced by mixing human need with divine promise, and the know-how to put the product on the street. It is a gift that managers of Christian organizations can acquire and develop because it is a gift that God desires to give.

CHAPTER FIVE

PRAY, PLAN, AND PUNT!

It was near the end of the first half in a high school football game; the home team was backed up against its own goal line and trailing in the score. The coach sent in the quarterback with the instructions: "Run three plays into the line and punt."

The first play gained two yards. On the second play, the halfback found an opening and advanced five more yards before being tackled. On the third play, the fullback broke through the line and ran the length of the field to the opponent's five yard line, where he was tackled. The coach ran down the sideline ready to call a new play and score a touchdown, only to see his quarterback line the team up in punt formation and kick the ball out of the end zone!

It was a good plan under the circumstances—run three line plays and punt! The quarterback executed the plan to perfection. From the standpoint of the larger objective, however, which was to score, the plan became obsolete the moment a new field situation developed. The original assumption was that the three running plays would not gain enough ground for a first down, and that a passing play was too great a risk in that situation. Lacking the instinct, or experience, to call a new play given the new situation, the quarterback faithfully followed the planned sequence.

This illustrates for us the importance of leadership in Christian organizations. An action plan is viable only for as long as the assumptions that called for it are valid. Some Christian organizations, I fear, operate on the basis of pray, plan, and punt! Once the operation has been committed to God in prayer, the plans are fortified by the assurance that they are "the will of God," and regardless of signs and evidences to the contrary, the execution of the plan will relentlessly take place—line up in punt formation!

What is distinctive about leadership, we have said in the

83

previous chapter, is the ability to read the signs of promise and translate them into specific goals. It is the relation between goal and promise that defines the role of leadership in an organization. This relation is dynamic, not fixed or static. For promise is itself not yet a goal.

The Jewish people lived by the promise of a Messiah. But they did not live out the promise in terms of a specific goal of recognizing and making way for the Messiah. Instead, the daily lives of the Jewish people, under the relentless tutelage of their religious leaders, became a routine operation—pray, plan, and punt.

It was John the Baptizer who read the promise in terms of an action plan related to the specific goal of "preparing the way of the Lord." He demonstrated a unique quality of leadership precisely because he was able to relate the promise to a goal, and thus had the discretionary freedom to recognize Jesus as the Messiah and to baptize him. The Jewish leaders, on the other hand, were already in their "punt formation," so to speak, and refused to see the signs of the promise in their midst. Here again, we see the distinction between the "leader" who is most concerned for the preservation of power and position, and the one who exercizes true leadership.

Our purpose in this chapter is to explore further the second aspect of leadership: directing and coordinating the energies and resources of the organization toward realization of the goals.

As we have seen, it is important for the organization to have specific goals derived from its mission statement. This statement is, in a sense, a goal statement. It is an interpretation of the promise and a translation of the vision into a statement of goals that identify the organization's central purpose for existence in the world, for the sake of the kingdom of God.

A primary task of leadership, therefore, is that of enabling the organization to create a mission statement that has a high degree of ownership on the part of the administrators and staff of the organization. We discussed this at the end of Chapter Three, where we said that the creative, ongoing task of relating promise to projections will keep Christian organizations open to the will of God at each phase of the administrative and decision-making process. We went on to suggest that discretionary leadership can be seen as an investment of the organization in its own mission statement. This task of leadership involves directing the life and resources of the organization in such a way that each member of the organization experiences to some degree a sense of accomplishing the will of God through the mission and work of God in the world. We are now ready to speak more fully and specifically of this task.

The concept of the will of God may be one of the most misunderstood and misused concepts in the vocabulary of Christian faith. Ordinarily, Christians assume that the first requirement in making a decision or undertaking a venture is to determine the will of God. If one understands this to be a process by which he or she can discover the will of God as a specific plan or decision that God has already made and that we need only to implement or follow, then confusion and frustration may well result.

Certainly we are encouraged to believe from God's Word that the proper *goal* for Christians is to do the will of God. This should also be true for Christian organizations. If, however, the will of God is the goal, and if the goal is the result of translating the signs of promise into an action plan, then the will of God is not itself the plan. Nor should we think that decisions that need to be made in order to achieve the goal are necessarily the will of God per se.

Consider the following scenario. Bill W. is the president of a Christian organization that has as its central mission the training of lay evangelists to spread the gospel among the unreached tribal people in central South America. The great commission in Matthew 28:19-20 was the scriptural mandate that led him to this vision. He determined, through study of Scripture, that the method God had ordained for the fulfillment of the great commission was that of seeking out key men from within an ethnic group and training them to evangelize their fellow countrymen, planting churches out of the newly converted believers.

Because he derived this method from his study of the Bible, and because he had sought from God a clear indication of his will as to a plan to reach these people, he concluded that his plan was itself ordained of God. Proceeding step by step, he made decisions as to the implementation of the plan on the basis that God's will was to be followed in every detail as the plan unfolded. This gave him tremendous assurance that the mission would be successful, and through communication of this vision and plan to Christian friends, he was able to raise sufficient financial support to set up a headquarters for his organization and hire a staff to begin the recruitment and training of the lay evangelists.

After two years of operation, the headquarters staff received a discouraging report from the field director. Not one lay evangelist had been trained and sent back to the field, though several converts had been made from which five prospects had been selected for training. In each case, those selected refused to return to their own people after attending the training sessions. According to the field director, they said that they were no longer accepted by their people. The field director concluded his report with the recommendation that the president hire an expert in missiology to evaluate the situation and come up with a method of evangelization and church planting that was more feasible for the cultural and ethnic situation in which they were working.

The president reacted strongly. "We cannot abandon a biblical method and be disobedient to the will of God," he told his staff. "The real problem is that we have failed to make disciples out of the converts that we have selected to be lay evangelists. If they were true disciples, they would go back to their own people and God would honor his Word. We need to strengthen the training program. I had better go down myself and take charge of the training." What Bill was really saying was, "Team, line up in punt formation!"

The will of God is not a plan or method that drops down out of heaven. Rather, it is related to the goal. Yes, it is certainly God's will that the gospel be proclaimed to every person. And yes, it is perfectly appropriate that a mission statement of a Christian organization translate this will of God into a specific goal. But the will of God is not itself the plan nor the specific decisions as to the best way to reach this goal. In the above scenario the confusion began with the misunderstanding of how God's will is related to the method and plan. Once the equation is made between the will of God and a specific decision or plan, leadership becomes paralyzed and what ought to be a very practical and wise change in strategy and method becomes spiritualized into an issue of obedience to the will of

God. One suspects that in cases like this, the matter also becomes one of spiritual crisis for the leader. To admit that the
method or plan is not working is to confess that one has not
been in the "center of God's will."

Our basic thesis in this chapter is that leadership is most
effective when it moves an organization *toward* the will of God
as a goal, and that the decisions and plans necessary to accomplish this are matters of human discretion and practical
wisdom. The will of God must always be in view as a goal, but
we are not ordinarily to think of it as a specific plan or method
that God has in mind and that we must then determine
through a direct spiritual "mind reading." Rather, as suggested in Chapter Three, the will of God is bound up in the
mission of the organization, not in the organization itself; it is
bound up in decision makers, not in the decision itself.[1]

The proper sequence to the will of God, according to our
understanding of the biblical paradigm, is that effective leadership begins by understanding the wisdom of God as pointing toward the goal, liberates the work of God through an
action plan that moves toward the goal, and finally experiences the will of God in the day-to-day execution of the plan.

We can represent this leadership paradigm as follows:

WISDOM OF GOD ——————— GOAL
WORK OF GOD ——————— ACTION PLAN
WILL OF GOD ——————— EXECUTION

In this paradigm the wisdom of God is the practical sense of
staying with his promise, which is attached to the specific goal.
The work of God is the effective agent that becomes manifest
through the outworking of the action plan. The plan releases
the power of God to work so that movement toward the goal is
made possible. The will of God is the realization of the goal,
which is itself an interpretation of promise. A good illustration
of this paradigm is the leadership of Joshua as he took over the
responsibility of leading the people of Israel into the promised
land.

1. This thesis is in general agreement with the approach taken by Garry
Friesen and J. Robin Maxson in their helpful book, *Decision Making and the
Will of God* (Portland, Ore.: Multnomah Press, 1980).

The Lord first sets forth the goal and counsels wisdom:

> Now therefore arise, go over this Jordan, you and all this peo-
> ple, into the land which I am giving to them [the goal] . . . as I
> promised to Moses. . . . Only be strong and very courageous,
> being careful to do according to all the law which Moses my
> servant commanded you; turn not from it to the right hand or
> to the left, that you may have good success wherever you go
> [wisdom]. (Josh. 1:2-3, 7)

Second, Joshua devised an action plan in which the work of
God would be directly implicated: he assembled the people at
the bank of the Jordan, the threshold to the promised land,
and told them,

> Sanctify yourselves; for tomorrow the Lord will do wonders
> among you. . . . Take up the ark of the covenant, and pass
> before the people . . . and when the soles of the feet of the
> priests who bear the ark of the Lord, the Lord of all the earth,
> shall rest in the waters of the Jordan, the waters of the Jordan
> shall be stopped from flowing. (Josh. 3:5-6, 13)

Third, the execution of the action plan took place, and the
people crossed over the Jordan into the promised land (Josh.
3:14–4:19). At this point the Lord revealed clearly that the
venture was accomplished according to his will, and he told
Joshua: "This day I have rolled away the reproach of Egypt
from you" (Josh. 5:9).

The paradigm of leadership we have sketched here suggests to us a model by which those who manage Christian
organizations can effectively direct and coordinate the energies and resources of the organization toward realization of
the goals as set forth in the mission statement. In the remainder of this chapter, we will develop this paradigm as it
relates to leadership for Christian organizations, using the
Epistle of James in the New Testament as a biblical basis for
this exposition.

THE WISDOM OF GOD: THE COMMON SENSE
OF LEADERSHIP

The Epistle of James is known for its practical and common-
sense approach to the Christian life. Yet James does not offer

practical advice in the place of genuine knowledge, nor does he suggest that doing good is a substitute for being good. Drawing upon the Hebrew concept of wisdom, he argues that the test of real knowledge is in the result that it produces when carried out into action.

"If any of you lacks wisdom," he writes, "let him ask God, who gives to all men generously and without reproaching, and it will be given him" (1:5). God is the source of true wisdom, says James, and so "every good endowment and every perfect gift is from above, coming down from the Father of lights" (1:17).

So, too, argues James, the test of wisdom and understanding is not a good theory, but a good life that is manifest in "the meekness of wisdom" (3:13). This wisdom from above is "pure, then peaceable, gentle, open to reason, full of mercy and good fruits, without uncertainty or insincerity. And the harvest of righteousness is sown in peace by those who make peace" (3:17-18).

We have suggested in our paradigm of leadership that the wisdom of God corresponds to what we call goals. James confirms this by showing that the true wisdom which comes from God is manifested in the result of actions, not merely in their intentions.

The Hebrew perspective on life did not first of all consist of an abstract theory of knowledge or of an abstract concept of action. Rather, the Hebrews contemplated the good as a goal in life to be achieved, and a plan of action was then conceived with the goal included in the action. This is quite different from, say, the Greek way of thinking. For the Greeks, reality is first of all an object of thought. Consequently, there is a tendency to abstract from the historical field of actions and consequences and to focus on truth as an ideal, as a reality that is first of all known to the mind. In this way of thinking, the *telos* or goal of an action lies outside of the action itself.

For example, a person may design a house and draw up a set of plans and specifications by which it is to be built. The builder works by the set of plans, what we call a blueprint. When he has finished, the builder's work is evaluated according to how closely he followed the plans, which clearly specify every dimension. The act of building is judged to be good if it follows the plan. The use made of the house and the character of the people who live in the house are not factors of concern to the builder. If he is a master craftsman, he will exercise the same scrupulous care in building a brothel as in building a temple. For him, the goal is completed when the building is constructed "according to plan."

This way of thinking is totally foreign to the Hebrew, who considers it total folly. For him the good is not a perfect design as an abstract blueprint to follow, but rather the quality of life that results from one's choices and actions. Because this quality of life is itself grounded in the character and will of God, it is a goal that has transcendent, or absolute, quality. But because it is also a goal that is promised and placed as the outcome of historical actions and decisions, it is a goal that is feasible and accessible through human decisions and actions.

More than that, for the Hebrew, plans and decisions are not measured in accordance with predetermined and abstract concepts of reality, but are measured in terms of how far they go toward realizing the goal. Thus, plans and human decisions are relative and not absolute. There is a clear dimension of freedom in making plans, for no plan or decision has to follow a blueprint, so to speak, but is judged to be either a wise or foolish plan according to whether or not it reaches the goal.

In the same way, God himself has freedom to "change his plans," even to "change his mind" without being in self-contradiction. The experience of Jonah is testimony to that! Also, we might recall the incident with Moses when Yahweh announced that he would no longer accompany the people of Israel, and instead would create a new people out of Moses. Through Moses' intercession, God changed that plan and said that he would indeed continue to accompany the people, though he would do so in a different way. And it is recorded that God "repented of the evil which he thought to do to his people" (Exod. 32:14).

This has always been a source of discomfort and even consternation to our way of thinking, as we tend to think more like the Greeks than like the Hebrews. For us, a plan is itself a reality, whereas for the Hebrews, it is only a way to get to the reality.

Furthermore, for the Hebrew thinking is never dissociated from actions as a concrete and historical reality. Consequently, the wise person is one who lives and acts in such a way that the outcome of his actions will be good rather than evil, substance rather than mere show. This is "good sense," and, in fact, is common sense.

With this background, we are ready to look at the implications of the wisdom of God for leadership in Christian organizations. Effective leadership, we have said, is reading the signs of promise and translating those signs into goals for the organization.

It is now quite clear that the issue is not whether an organization has goals, but how these goals are derived, and how they are related to the wisdom of God. In the example cited above, the builder of the house had his goal—to complete the house according to plan. In this case, the goal is itself determined by the plan, and the plan is first of all an abstract idea—a mental image or design. There is a form of leadership that proceeds along these lines. What we see as the fatal flaw in such a leadership style is the fact that the goals of an organization can be so identified with the design—that is, the organizational plan—that there is no freedom to alter the plan for the sake of the good, as determined by the wisdom of God.

It would not be difficult to find examples of this. We could think of a pastor who exercises his leadership of the church in such a way that the goal of building a successful program, not to mention an imposing edifice, becomes so demanding that the congregation is thrown into spiritual confusion and chaos, and the pastor's family destroyed in the process. But he met his goal! Or, we could think of the head of a Christian organization who establishes ten-year goals for the organization in terms of institutional survival and management efficiency, while in the meantime depriving the employees and staff of dignity and human value, not to mention contributing to an erosion of the sense of Christian community.

Is it not clear that such a leadership style, even with the most rigorous management procedures for long-range planning, goal setting, and cost control efficiency, falls short of reaching the goal that "comes down from above" and is "full of mercy and good fruits" (Jas. 3:17)? Does not common sense alone tell us that something is wrong with such a management process?

Once more I need to make it clear that I am not suggesting that the wisdom of God and "common sense" are substitutes for planning, goal setting, and good management practices. I hope it is clear by now that Christian organizations must first establish goals, which are to be fashioned out of an interpretation of the promise of God in terms of attainable and feasible results of human decisions and actions. These goals will then serve as criteria by which planning and goal setting as a regular process of management take place.

The effect of creating a leadership style out of this paradigm is that the management process of Christian organizations becomes opened up to the "good sense" that issues from the wisdom of God. There will be a freedom both to make and to change plans without catastrophic results for the organization and personal failure for those who manage it. Because the good of the people who serve in the organization is also included in its goal, which is an interpretation of God's wisdom, these people are not subject to the plan; rather, the plan is subject to the good of these people. If this was the case when Moses, knowing that God's wisdom included the destiny of the people of Israel, interceded with God, even so it is the case with Christian organizations.

Let us summarize the points we have made in viewing the wisdom of God as the common sense of leadership:

1. The wisdom of God views the outcome of human actions and decisions as the goal toward which these actions move.

2. The responsibility of those who provide leadership for Christian organizations is to develop a mission statement for the organization that translates God's promise through Jesus Christ into goals for the organization that will determine both the purpose and the character of the organization.

3. The decisions and plans that managers of Christian organizations make are relative to the goals of the organization as set forth in the mission statement, and are never infallible or unchangeable in themselves.

4. The specific objectives by which the organization is managed are part of the "management plan" and must be tested against the perceived outcome as defined by the stated goals.

5. It is the specific responsibility of those who provide leadership to keep the goals, as representing the wisdom of God, uppermost in the management strategy, thus preserving both the purpose and the character of the organization.

6. Leadership in a Christian organization is, then, a process

of management by "common sense," for the wisdom of God is the most sensible of all wisdom.

THE WORK OF GOD: THE CREATIVE POWER OF LEADERSHIP

In our paradigm of leadership, following the wisdom of God, which correlates with the goals of a Christian organization, is the work of God, which correlates with what we have called action plans. In developing the paradigm further, we now will explore the work of God as the creative power of leadership.

Again we turn to the Epistle of James as a biblical basis for exploring this aspect of the paradigm. "What does it profit," asks James, "if a man says he has faith but has not works?" (2:14). It is the wise and understanding person, he says, who will "show his works in the meekness of wisdom" (2:13). James warns against anger because it does not "work the righteousness of God" (1:20). Consequently, he concludes, "faith by itself, if it has no works, is dead" (2:17).

James's logic is clearly evident in terms of his basic premise that the wisdom of God is manifest in a "harvest of righteousness" (3:14). The creative power of God is not a "potential" that exists as a static and lifeless possibility, but it is manifest always as a "work of God" in actuality. In the case of God, actuality precedes possibility. It is possible for him to work because he has already worked. To conceive of God, then, as a sheer object of faith, is "dead faith" because it is not based on the reality of God that is manifest through his works.

"My Father is working still," said Jesus, "and I am working" (John 5:17). On another occasion, he said: "We must work the works of him who sent me, while it is day; night comes, when no one can work" (John 9:4). Following that statement, he healed the man who had been blind from birth. This clearly was meant to be a direct association between his own ministry and the work of God the Father.

Since this healing took place on the Sabbath, we also see here the creative power of the work of God. It is one thing for the blind man to be healed. This is itself a creative work. But it is another thing for it to be done on the Sabbath, when work was forbidden, and where the sanctions against work were interpreted by the Jews as a plan of God for all ages. Once more we see that to the Jews the plan was also the goal. To keep the law was of more significance than to heal the man. Jesus demonstrated the creative power of leadership not in breaking the law but by interpreting and fulfilling the law in terms of God's redemptive promise. To all but those who had bound up the goal in the law itself, it made perfect sense that God should have as his goal the liberation of the blind man from his condition. The healing as a work of God thus manifested the wisdom of God.

James has a clear view of this creative power that works the righteousness of God. It is the "perfect" law, "the law of liberty," and he who looks into this law perseveres, for "being no hearer that forgets but a doer that acts, he shall be blessed in his doing" (1:25). We must keep in mind that James first discusses the wisdom of God as the source of every perfect gift. Only then does he say that faith is manifest by works. Not just any kind of activity is blessed of God, but only that action which releases the work of God—which is the work by which faith is made alive.

Clearly, this has implications for a style of leadership for Christian organizations. Faith apart from works is dead. We can look at this in the following way: The goals established by the mission statement of a Christian organization translate the promise of God into outcomes of human actions and decisions. The organization is now committed, as its central purpose, to the realization of these goals. In a sense, these goals are also "faith statements," for it is by faith in the living God who "is working" that the organization believes that its work will be the work of God.

Without clearly defined action plans designed to achieve the stated goals, the mission statement is "dead," to use the terminology of James. The role of leadership in managing a Christian organization is not finished with the establishment of a statement of goals that embody the promise of God. Effective leadership will now understand that clearly developed action plans serve as the creative edge of the work of God. These plans actually unleash the power of God to work through human agencies and instrumentality.

This is the inner logic of the incarnation of God in Jesus Christ. In becoming human, God did not surrender his divine power; rather, he unleashed his power through the human actions and instrumentality of Jesus. We are authorized to make a direct identification between the human work of Jesus and the divine work of God, because Jesus is not only truly human but fully God. Through the power of the resurrected Jesus, as administered by the Holy Spirit in the lives of believing Christians, human decisions and actions can now be the means by which this same power is unleashed as the work of God.

As a result, we see that human decisions and actions can themselves be liberated from their powerlessness and ineffectiveness to work the work of God. This means that the means and methods by which Christian organizations unleash this power of God through action plans are basically neutral, neither good nor evil in themselves. There are not certain methods and means that are intrinsically spiritual while others are basically secular. All are secular and powerless until they are brought into the service of the wisdom of God and become the manifestation of the work of God.

Some managers of Christian organizations are uncertain about this, and may tend to give a higher priority to "faith alone" over any action plan using a secular method. Earlier I referred to the ambivalence of those who trust God to bring in the necessary money to finance the mission through "faith and prayer alone." These same leaders are not hesitant to use modern audiovisual technology to spread the word that it is through prayer and faith that God works. Meanwhile, they also rely upon the services of the government postal service to deliver the money to their door!

There ought to be no such ambivalence nor such a false spiritual dichotomy on the part of the leadership of Christian organizations who understand the biblical paradigm we have been developing. The creative power of leadership is in selecting the most effective means by which the goals of the organization can be achieved. Jesus used dirt mixed with saliva on at least one occasion to heal the eyes of a blind man. On other occasions he reached out and touched the person to whom he was ministering. And on at least one other occasion, at the request of a centurion whose servant was paralyzed, he simply spoke the word and the servant was healed without Jesus seeing or talking with him (Matt. 8:5-13). These illustrations, of course, only suggest to us that it is not the method nor the means but the creative power of the work of God unleashed through those means that realizes the goal that embodies the promise.

What, then, is the critical test for methods and means? Precisely what we have already set forth: the wisdom of God that has been incorporated into goals for the organization. These goals necessarily include criteria that uphold the character of the organization in its ethical and spiritual integrity. If they do not, the goals are inadequately formulated, and leadership has failed at a crucial point.

Effective leadership means a creative and continual discovery of means and methods that unleash the power of God through action plans designed to accomplish the goals of the organization. This same leadership is charged with the responsibility for evaluating these means and methods on the basis of criteria developed out of the wisdom of God. In this way, effective leadership both liberates the management process to its most efficient and effective level and holds the process accountable to the goals as embodying the wisdom of God.

We can now summarize the points we have made concerning the work of God as the creative power of leadership:

1. The wisdom of God takes form as the specific goals of the organization developed in its mission statement.

2. The creative power of leadership is manifested in the development of action plans that unleash the power of God to move the organization toward realization of its goals.

3. The means and methods incorporated into the action plan are chosen in accordance with their effectiveness in moving the organization toward the goals as developed in the mission statement.

4. The work of God becomes measurable and capable of critical affirmation through the effectiveness of the action plan as related to the goals.

5. The role of leadership is expressed through creative development of action plans that incorporate the most effective progress toward realization of the goals.

6. The responsibility of leadership is to keep in view the goals, as expressive of the wisdom of God, as a check against

inefficient methods and means, as well as a check against methods and means that are contrary to the wisdom of God.

THE WILL OF GOD: THE CONSUMMATION OF LEADERSHIP

In our paradigm of leadership, the will of God is the final determination of the effectiveness of leadership, not the first principle by which leadership operates. It must also be said, of course, that the will of God must always be in view as the ultimate measure of that which is the work and wisdom of God. What is essential, however, is to understand that the will of God is not a blueprint that exists prior to human decision and action. Rather, the will of God is the consummation of all human endeavor and the benediction upon all human effort.

For this reason, we now turn to the third and final aspect of our paradigm for leadership: The will of God as the consummation of leadership.

After setting forth the wisdom of God as that which comes from above and determines the good outcome or goal of human choices and actions, James then shows how the work of God carries out this wisdom by moving toward the good through human actions. But James also discusses the will of God in the context of the freedom of human persons to set goals and to make action plans.

> Come now, you who say, "Today or tomorrow we will go into such and such a town and spend a year there and trade and get gain"; whereas you do not know about tomorrow. What is your life? For you are a mist that appears for a little time and then vanishes. Instead you ought to say, "If the Lord wills, we shall live and we shall do this or that." (Jas. 4:13-15)

What James warns against is the attitude that one can act with the arrogance and presumption that one's own plans and decisions are absolutely determinative of the good. Only God is absolutely good, and only he sovereignly determines what shall abide. Our own life is fraught with failures and fenced in with the finite limits of our own wisdom and power. We may think that we are full of power and knowledge when we make our decisions and plans. But we are not. We cannot control events that can easily lead to the overthrow of our plans, and we cannot protect ourselves from our own finite wisdom and sinful presumption.

Nonetheless, James does not suggest that it is wrong to make plans. It is only when we invest the will of God in our own decisions and plans that we are in danger of foolish presumption. The will of God is reserved for God's final benediction and blessing upon our efforts. This can be eagerly anticipated and earnestly sought, but it cannot be made a matter of presumption.

This has the effect of freeing our decisions and action plans from having to be accomplished in the way and form that we intended. This also frees us to adjust our decisions and plans as we continue to anticipate and seek the goal that is the measure of the wisdom of God, and will bring the validation that we have done the will of God. James sounds a note of hopeful patience with respect to the will of God:

> Be patient, therefore, brethren, until the coming of the Lord. Behold, the farmer waits for the precious fruit of the earth, being patient over it until it receives the early and the late rain. You also be patient. Establish your hearts, for the coming of the Lord is at hand. . . . You have heard of the steadfastness of Job, and you have seen the purpose of the Lord, how the Lord is compassionate and merciful. (5:7-8, 11)

When the work has been done in the wisdom of God, there is good reason to be confident that it will also have been done in the will of God. Thus, the will of God is not a way of making human decisions and actions "fail-safe," so to speak; rather, it is the confidence we can have in our own efforts precisely because God wills that our work shall also be his work, and that our labor will result in a harvest of his own righteousness.

The apostle Paul is a consistent model of leadership with respect to the paradigm of the wisdom of God, the work of God, and the will of God. He is invariably moving toward goals that he has set as a realistic interpretation of the promise of God. These goals include not only targeted objectives with respect to planting new churches, but also genuine concern for the welfare of those on his team and those who respond to his ministry. What is equally impressive is the freedom Paul has to create action plans, make decisions, select from several alternatives, and make modifications and adjustments without once questioning the matter of the will of God in his life.

When Paul arrived in Athens following his ministry at Thessalonica, he was worried over how the church would hold up under persecution; in his letter to the Thessalonians he explains how he decided to send Timothy to them: "Therefore when we could bear it no longer, we were willing to be left behind at Athens alone, and we sent Timothy, our brother" (1 Thess. 3:1-2). Paul did not say that he received a direct indication as to God's will in this matter, but simply said, "we were willing."

In writing to the Philippian church, Paul says: "I have thought it necessary to send to you Epaphroditus my brother and fellow worker" (Phil. 2:25). Again, Paul indicates that this plan was devised out of his reading of the situation rather than some direct revelation from God.

On one occasion at least, Paul interpreted a situation as particularly advantageous for his ministry, and even said that when he came to Troas "a door was opened for me in the Lord" (2 Cor. 2:12). He went on immediately, however, to tell the Corinthians that "my mind could not rest because I did not find my brother Titus there. So I took leave of them and went on to Macedonia" (2:13). Paul appeared to feel that a strategic opportunity to minister the gospel was only one option for him to consider in making his plans. "Open doors" and "closed doors" for him were not themselves infallible evidences of God's will, but factors that led him to take actions he felt sure would lead to doing God's will.

These are but a few examples of the way in which Paul exercised freedom in making his decisions and plans in accordance with the circumstances but always with the confidence that he would be found within the will of God in the end. In a passage that speaks clearly of his own apostolic credentials, and yet warns against presuming that the will and commendation of God can be claimed on one's own behalf, Paul wrote:

> This is how one should regard us, as servants of Christ and stewards of the mysteries of God. Moreover it is required of stewards that they be found trustworthy. But with me it is a very small thing that I should be judged by you or by any human

court. I do not even judge myself. I am not aware of anything
against myself, but I am not thereby acquitted. It is the Lord
who judges me. Therefore do not pronounce judgment before
the time, before the Lord comes, who will bring to light the
things now hidden in darkness and will disclose the purposes of
the heart. Then every man will receive his commendation from
God. (1 Cor. 4:1-5)

The outcome of all decisions is obviously determined ultimately by God's sovereign will. But, as Garry Friesen helpfully
points out, "for all practical purposes, *sovereign guidance has no
direct bearing on the conscious considerations* of the decision
maker."[2] The attempt to make decisions based on a direct
identification between the sovereign will of God and these
decisions cannot really be carried out consistently in every area
and detail of life. There is no basis for determining which
decisions out of the multitude of decisions made by every person and by every Christian organization ought to be determined directly by God's sovereign will. All decisions and all
human actions take place in the arena of freedom and responsibility that God has granted to us; but all of these decisions are
also to be made with the understanding that they ultimately
stand under the control of God's sovereign will. This is the
point James is making in the passage cited above (5:7-8).

The basis on which Paul seemed to operate is what Friesen
calls the "principle of spiritual expediency."[3] The spiritual
factor in decision making is bound up in the wisdom of God,
which we have said is interpreted as the goal toward which our
decisions and action plans move. The principle of expediency
suggests that decisions and plans that most effectively accomplish this goal are the best ones. This is why it is often most
expedient to change plans or to reverse a decision when the
goal is not being reached. For those who identify decisions and
plans directly with the will of God, however, it will be: pray,
plan, and punt!

We have made several points in discussing the will of God as
the consummation of leadership:

2. Ibid., p. 233.
3. Ibid., p. 187.

1. Human decisions and actions move toward the will of God, and seek fulfillment in the will of God.

2. The will of God is a sovereign will, which means that it is the ultimate determination of the good.

3. No human decision or action is ordinarily expected to be dictated by God in advance through his sovereignty—though we should be open to exceptions, as James points out.

4. Effective leadership has the freedom to make decisions and action plans on the basis of spiritual expediency—that which seems best in the circumstances in light of the goal, which is the wisdom of God.

We began our discussion of this paradigm of leadership by looking at the way in which Joshua set out to bring the people of Israel into the promised land. The execution of his action plan led to the consummation of his leadership in a celebration of the will of God. When the last of the people had crossed over the Jordan, and the waters of the river had closed in behind them, Joshua led the people in a ritual of memorial and renewal. Twelve stones were taken out of the riverbed and set up at Gilgal as a testimony to the fulfillment of God's promise that "all of the peoples of the earth" may know that the hand of the Lord is mighty (Josh. 4:23-24). Joshua then led the people in a ritual of renewal and celebration. The people who had been born during the forty years in the wilderness had not yet been circumcized, so this was done as a renewal of the covenant promise. Then the people celebrated the festival of the Passover, and on the very next day "they ate of the produce of the land, unleavened cakes and parched grain. And the manna ceased on the morrow, when they ate of the produce of the land" (5:10-12).

The goal had been reached. The promise had been fulfilled; the will of God had been accomplished. This is the consummation of leadership. It includes a celebration of God's will accomplished and the renewal of the people in the covenant relation to God and to one another.

Oh, yes, there is a postscript to the high school football game. During the halftime, the coach had a talk with the quarterback, and told him that he had the freedom to call his own play if the situation ever came up again when he had the opportunity to score. And he did. On the last play of the game he called for a draw play in a passing situation, and they won the game. There was a victory celebration in the locker room afterward.

But that, of course, was just a football game. Christian organizations know very little of rituals and festivals where leadership is consummated in celebration. Perhaps they could learn from others.

CHAPTER SIX

A CASE FOR EXCELLENCE IN CHRISTIAN ORGANIZATIONS

Above and beyond our likes and dislikes—years of experience or freshness of approach—egos and ambitions—lie the most important factors—love for art and respect for quality work.

In order for art to remain strong and viable as an expressive avenue among so much visual glut—it must have power, vision, energy, courage and integrity. Set up your own perimeters—choose your weapons, clarify your aims and sing.

(Josine Ianco-Starrels)

The apostle Paul could sing it: "Whatever is true, whatever is honorable, whatever is just, whatever is pure, whatever is lovely, whatever is gracious, if there is any excellence, if there is anything worthy of praise, think about these things" (Phil. 4:8).

Most of us would be hard pressed to define *excellence*. It surely has something to do with both art and ethics. The word suggests the discipline that is disguised in freedom through which a thing is created in such a way that one could hardly imagine that it could be better than it is. A mother may gush with extravagant praise over the drawing her six-year-old brings home from his first art class in school—but it is Michelangelo's paintings on the ceiling of the Sistine Chapel that command our silence and our awe: this is excellence.

Yet we have not touched the core of excellence as understood by the Hebrews and as suggested in the life and spirit of Jesus. For the people of Israel the work of God was excellent and beyond compare. The mighty works of creation caused the Psalmist to sing the majesty and excellence of God (Ps. 8).

His deeds of mercy in covenant love are praised for being glorious and excellent (Ps. 36:7; Isa. 12:5; 28:29). Even the people themselves, as God's chosen ones, manifested a quality of excellence as those who consecrated human passion and life in bearing the name of God. So the philosopher Nietzsche could say of these people:

> In the Jewish "Old Testament," . . . there are human beings, things, and speeches in so grand a style that Greek and Indian literature have nothing to compare with it. With terror and reverence one stands before these tremendous remnants of what man once was. . . . The taste for the Old Testament is a touchstone for "great" and "small." . . . The dignity of death and a kind of *consecration* of passion has perhaps never yet been represented more beautifully . . . than by certain Jews of the Old Testament; to these even the Greeks could have gone to school![1]

In the New Testament, the touchstone for excellence is found in Jesus Christ, the single human person in whom the fullness of deity dwells bodily (Col. 2:9). This is true despite the fulfillment in his life and death of the dreadful prophecy of Isaiah: "he had no form or comeliness that we should look at him, and no beauty that we should desire him" (Isa. 53:2). The criteria of both art and ethics fail at precisely the point that the work of excellence was taking place through the incarnate and crucified form of God in Jesus Christ.

We are shown here, as Paul so eloquently sang in his hymn of love, a "more excellent way"—the way of love itself. Divine love, poured out through the life and work of Jesus, is the touchstone for excellence. Excellence is now a quality of being more than an artistic representation and form of life. Yes, this quality of life inspires human persons to strive for excellence in form through all the repertoire of the arts, but true excellence is a *way* of life before it can be a *form* of life.

There are intimations of this excellence even among the followers of Jesus. Matthew records one such occasion near the end of Jesus' life when he was at Bethany. A woman came in while he and his disciples were gathered at the table for a meal, and poured an alabaster flask of expensive oil over his

1. F. Nietzsche, *Beyond Good and Evil*, sec. 52.

head in a ritual of anointment. The disciples were indignant and rebuked her for this "waste." Jesus, however, said: "Why do you trouble the woman? For she has done a beautiful thing to me. . . . Wherever this gospel is preached in the whole world, what she has done will be told in memory of her" (Matt. 26:6-13). This is excellence.

Why this excursus on the nature of excellence? Because it is our purpose in this chapter to make a case for excellence in Christian organizations.

In Chapter Four we said that effective leadership means reading the signs of God's promise in the context of present events, and translating these signs into goals. We saw in Chapter Five that effective leadership means directing and coordinating the energies and resources of the organization toward realization of the goals. Now, in this chapter, we want to show that effective leadership of Christian organizations means maintaining quality control over the character and purpose of the organization; this is to "give proof before the churches" of love and obedience to Christ (2 Cor. 8:24).

Despite the fact that the apostle Paul was a visionary leader and systematic organizer of people into churches and tasks, the thing that appeared to cause him the most pain was the people's failure to exhibit love and human compassion in their dealings with each other. He was obviously upset by those who practiced and taught what he considered to be contrary to the gospel. He minced no words in labeling them as enemies of Christ and warned the churches to avoid them at all costs. Yet Paul did not make conformity to doctrinal truths the highest criterion of excellence.

In his first letter to Timothy, who is apparently responsible for giving leadership to the church at Ephesus, he warned against "certain persons" who were teaching a "different doctrine," and reminded Timothy that "the aim of our charge is love that issues from a pure heart and a good conscience and sincere faith" (1 Tim. 1:3-5). Paul then provides a partial list of offenses against love, which includes "the unholy and profane, . . . manslayers, immoral persons, sodomites, kidnapers, liars, perjurers." Paul concludes this list by saying, "and whatever else is contrary to sound doctrine, in accordance with the glorious gospel of the blessed God with which I have been entrusted" (1:9-11).

What scandalized Paul, and caused him grief and pain, was the failure of his churches to walk in love. To the Corinthians he writes appealing for unity and humility, reminding them that they are saints, "God's temple" where the Spirit of God dwells (1 Cor. 3:16). In scolding them for their unseemly practice in their love feasts where the Lord's Supper is celebrated, he says that they have not come together for the better but for the worse (11:17). And it was in their contentious exercise of the spiritual gifts that he saw their greatest failure, and so penned his "hymn of love" as the "more excellent way" (12:31–13:13).

In his letter to the Galatians he accused them of being "bewitched" (3:1) and of having lost the freedom of life in the Spirit for slavery to the law. And so he pleads with them to "walk by the Spirit" rather than by the flesh, and so manifest the fruit of the Spirit: love, joy, peace, patience, kindness, goodness, faithfulness, gentleness, and self-control (5:16, 22-23).

The point is this. The character of a Christian organization is rooted in its quality of life as measured by the love of God in Christ displayed in the basic human and personal relations that constitute the daily life of the organization as a community. This thesis controls our discussion of excellence as a characteristic of Christian organizations.

Of course, we are making two assumptions here; first, that the organization has a statement of its basic Christian beliefs that is biblically based and faithful to the revealed truth of God. By this the organization confesses what it believes to be true with regard to God and his revealed Word and gospel. Second, we are assuming that the organization has a statement of its own mission and purpose, which translates the wisdom and promise of God into specific goals to determine the plans and objectives of the organization. By this the organization confesses what it is about as an organization with an existence and purpose in the world.

But this is not enough. It is not yet the "way of excellence" as exemplified by Christ and as taught by the apostle Paul. There is a third "confession" every Christian organization must make, in addition to its confessions as to what it believes and what it is about. This is the confession it makes by virtue of the character of its life as an organization.

I do not mean to suggest that every Christian organization is a community in the sense that a local parish church is a community of Christ. In Chapter Two we saw how the Christian organization as a paraparochial form of the church has a "limited liability" with respect to the care of its members. The members of a paraparochial Christian organization are expected to be members of a parochial form of the church, as well, where there is a more or less "unlimited liability" of the community for each member.

Christian organizations may not be the community of the body of Christ in precisely the same way that the local church exists as a community of Christ. Nonetheless, a Christian organization represents the presence of Christ through the life of its members and through the function of these persons in the organization. This is why the apostle Paul was so concerned about the *character* of the project to raise relief funds for the Jerusalem church, in addition to his concern about the *purpose* of the project. "We intend that no one should blame us about this liberal gift which we are administering, for we aim at what is honorable not only in the Lord's sight but also in the sight of men" (2 Cor. 8:20-21).

The frequent admonitions in the New Testament concerning the practice of love as an indispensable element of Christian community do not leave Christian organizations exempt. For Christian organizations are under the same twofold mandate as is any form of the body of Christ: to uphold the basic value of human persons as created in the image of God, and to embody the life and character of Jesus Christ in every action and relationship. "Do good to all men, and especially those who are of the household of faith" (Gal. 6:10). "Let the peace of Christ rule in your hearts. . . . Let the word of Christ dwell in you richly. . . . And whatever you do, in word or deed, do everything in the name of the Lord Jesus, giving thanks to God the Father through him" (Col. 3:15–17).

We need to stress this "third confession" because Christian organizations have not always been noted for the quality of life experienced on the part of those who work in the organization. Nor have Christian organizations always been careful to "do good to all men" by upholding basic human values in their dealing with those outside the organization.

Christian organizations should take careful note of the research and conclusions presented by Thomas Peters and Robert Waterman in their book, *In Search of Excellence*.[2] In citing the top ten organizations in the country, based upon their criteria of sustained financial performance, innovation, and productivity, they found that each one demonstrated the common practice of "paying positive attention" to people in the organization.[3] "Every person seeks meaning," argued Peters and Waterman, as well as recognition as persons.[4] For this reason, they concluded that the companies receiving high marks for excellence were the same companies noted for their recognition of the quality of life on the part of their staff and workers.

If secular organizations are discovering that "paying positive attention" to human persons also produces excellence, we can well understand why this is so from a Christian perspective. As Christians, we have different reasons for suggesting that excellence is keyed to basic human values. Excellence is rooted in God's love for human persons. He demonstrated this by first of all creating them with the positive value of possessing his own image and likeness, and then by giving his Son, Jesus Christ, to redeem and restore that human image through the same gracious, divine love. What is difficult to understand is why Christian organizations have seldom been noted for exhibiting that same mark of excellence demonstrated by some secular organizations.

Perhaps it is because zeal for the kingdom of God understood primarily as purpose and task has blinded Christian organizations to the marks of the kingdom that are meant to be exhibited in the lives of those working for the kingdom. The gospel of the kingdom is also a gospel of human values and human relationships in community. This ought to have been the first lesson learned from Jesus.

Thus far we have attempted to expound the basic thesis of this chapter: the character of a Christian organization is rooted in its quality of life as measured by the love of God in Christ displayed in the basic human and personal relations that constitute the daily life of the organization as a community. We

2. T. Peters and R. Waterman, *In Search of Excellence* (New York: Harper & Row, 1982).
3. Ibid., p. 94.
4. Ibid., p. 83.

will now apply this thesis to Christian organizations and develop several "marks of excellence" by which the character and quality of Christian organizations can be developed and sustained through effective leadership.

"Love does no wrong to a neighbor," writes the apostle Paul; "therefore love is the fulfilling of the law" (Rom. 13:10). In this simple statement we can find the basis for excellence as the outworking of love. First, we can state it in the negative form of what it is to "do wrong" to a neighbor. Love does not do wrong because 1) love does not defraud others to advance its own cause; 2) love does not exploit others for its own gain; 3) love does not fail others in their time of need; and 4) love does not deprive others of their full share in the enterprise.

"Doing wrong," then, is to defraud, exploit, fail, and deprive our neighbors. Jesus taught us that our neighbor is not only the one who belongs to our own group, but anyone with whom we have contact on the "road of life" (Luke 10:25-37). But "doing wrong" is the negative side of excellence.

There is a positive side to excellence, and the marks of excellence are the evidences of love for the neighbor. Let us consider four such marks as they are related to Christian organizations.

EXCELLENCE AS ETHICAL INTEGRITY

The Christian church has been plagued since its early days by what many view as a false dichotomy between the sacred and the profane. In the fifth century, Augustine gave classic statement to this view in his book, *The City of God*. Augustine sharply distinguished the City of God, as a sacred sphere of life, from the City of this World, which is fallen and outside of the sphere of God's grace. For Augustine, the spiritual integrity of dedication to God within the sphere of salvation had priority over any attempt for moral integrity apart from God's grace.

Consequently, Augustine could say: "Even our virtue in this life, genuine as it is because it is referred to the true goal of every good, lies more in the pardoning of sins than in any perfection of virtues."[5] The practical effect of this separation

5. Augustine, *City of God*, Bk. XIX, chap. 27.

of true spirituality from true morality was to create an ethical
integrity out of the spiritual mission of the church that tended
to dismiss the common ground rules for moral integrity as
hopelessly mired in the lost spiritual state of the world that lies
outside of God's saving grace.

Without consciously following such a sophisticated philosophy of spiritual virtue as Augustine advocated, many Christian organizations today operate on the same pragmatic
spiritual ethic. It works like this: The world is estranged from
God and in the service of the Devil. The mandate of the gospel
is to save human souls from sin and to baptize them into the
true community of Christ. This spiritual goal justifies whatever means are needed to accomplish God's saving purpose.
But to "play by the rules" the world has set up serves the
purpose of evil and not the purpose of God.

For example, should the District Attorney representing a
civil law enforcement agency be permitted to have access to the
financial records of a Christian television station that is "proclaiming the gospel"? According to one such Christian organization in Los Angeles County, the answer was No! And in
defiance of such legal attempts to examine their records, the
station finally was forced to suspend operations—not without
claiming persecution of Christians on the part of the state, of
course.

The distinction between that which is "of the world" and
that which is "of God" is absolute. Jesus made that clear in
teaching his disciples that he "was not of the world" nor were
they to be of this world (John 17). When faced with an attempt
to suppress their testimony to the risen Christ, the early disciples did not have to struggle with ethical complexities, but
simply replied, "We must obey God rather than men" (Acts
5:28).

It would be a mistake, however, to assume from this that
God has separated the spiritual mandate from the moral mandate. The moral mandate is grounded in the fundamental
character of what it is to be human—created in the image and
likeness of God. Biblical anthropology will not permit a separation of human persons into spiritual entities on the one hand
and moral agents on the other. Nor will it permit a dichotomy
between "saving souls" and honoring the moral conventions
of human society.

All human persons are the "neighbors" of God, and Jesus made no distinction between people—they were all objects of divine love. Love does no wrong to a neighbor, wrote Paul. And this means that love will not defraud one's neighbor, whether or not that neighbor is a Christian, for the sake of advancing the cause of a Christian organization. One may have to suffer persecution for honoring God in testifying to his love for all through Jesus Christ. But if one goes to jail for defrauding one's neighbor under the claim that proclaiming the gospel exempts one from such an ethical responsibility, there can be no defense on Christian grounds.

This is why the apostle Paul made such a point of saying that the means and method by which the funds were raised and delivered to the Jerusalem church must be done with ethical integrity. "We aim at what is honorable," he wrote, "not only in the Lord's sight but also in the sight of men" (2 Cor. 8:21). In writing to the Roman Christians, who certainly were not under a friendly governing authority in the person of Caesar, Paul urged them to be subject to the civil authorities not only to avoid God's wrath on the wrongdoer but also "for the sake of conscience." And then he continued by showing precisely what the content of a Christian conscience should be in this case by saying: "For this reason you also pay taxes, for the authorities are ministers of God, attending to this very thing. Pay all of them their dues, taxes to whom taxes are due, revenue to whom revenue is due, respect to whom respect is due, honor to whom honor is due" (Rom. 13:5-7).

What has been said above should be fairly obvious. Christian organizations are under the mandate of love to perform with ethical integrity and not to defraud legitimate governments and civil authorities of that which is rightly due to them. In the same way, Christian organizations are under the same mandate of love not to defraud others with whom they do business, nor their own constituency, for the sake of advancing their own spiritual cause.

Who among us is not appalled when we hear the all-too-common horror stories from secular contractors who no longer will do job work for Christian organizations without payment in advance? When asked, they will say it is because they have lost too much money on Christians. And when pressed further, they often report that when a Christian organization becomes delinquent in making payments, they are told not to worry, because "we are trusting the Lord" to bring in the money. One such "entrepreneur" of a Christian organization who made a practice of running up bills and not paying them actually told me that he believed that all of the money in the world belonged to the Lord, and securing services from the world without making payment was just one way of getting what belonged to the Lord anyway.

All of this ought to be quite clear and should need no further discussion to make the point. The way of excellence for Christian organizations includes ethical integrity in all dealings with those both outside of and within the constituency of the organization. Love does no wrong to one's neighbors—it does not defraud them on the pretext of a spiritual mission.

What is perhaps not so obvious, but of equal concern, is my conviction that inadequate or sloppy management practices on the part of Christian organizations are also a form of defrauding one's neighbor. We may not instinctively think of it in that way, but poor and ineffective management of an organization is also a lapse of ethical integrity. An organization exists as a way of expending and directing the human resources of time, energy, and usually money. Those who contribute to an organization by supporting it or working within it have made an investment of their own lives, faith, and resources in the organization. Managers of Christian organizations are, in a sense, managing an investment portfolio on behalf of all of those who are part of the organization, directly or indirectly.

As an example of what I mean here, we can look at Paul's letter to the Philippian church as a kind of "report to the stockholders." The Christians in Philippi, says Paul, have been the only ones to contribute regularly and directly to his own support. "You Philippians yourselves know that in the beginning of the gospel, when I left Macedonia, no church entered into partnership with me in giving and receiving except you only" (4:15). Earlier in his letter he refers to a gift from them carried to him by Epaphroditus, who risked his own life "to complete your service to me" (2:30). He also explains to them that the recent events in his life—his trip to Jerusalem, his subsequent two-year imprisonment in Caesarea, and now his two-year imprisonment in Rome—have "really served to advance the gospel" (1:12). Paul recognizes that their investment in him and in his ministry requires an accounting as to his stewardship of the gospel.

From this we can extrapolate the point that I am making. Ineffective and inefficient management practices defraud the neighbors who have invested their resources of time, energy, and financial support in the organization.

Some Christian organizations are no doubt seriously undermanaged. This can easily happen when the leadership fails to take account of the complexity of the organization's operations when it has made rapid and significant growth. Often in the early days of an organization, leadership is a "hands on" type of operation, with decision making, planning, and accounting all issuing out of one central office, and a good deal of "oral tradition" serving to carry forward standard policies and practices. With rapid growth and increasing complexity of operations, however, the organization becomes increasingly inefficient. This may be manifested by confusion and disorganization in handling routine accounting and office procedures, conflict and disorientation within the operational staff due to breakdown of communication, heavy turnover of staff due to low morale and lack of training procedures, and serious mistakes in allocating funds and in cost accounting due to lack of planning and budget control of all operations.

Another cause of undermanagement in a Christian organization may be the suspicion that management is unspiritual. There may be resistance to using better management practices out of a vague sense of uneasiness with the concept of management itself. Or there may be a more overt reliance on spiritual intuition, the leading of the Holy Spirit, and prayer rather than on techniques of management. These factors will be discussed in more depth in the final chapter of this book.

On the other hand, some Christian organizations may be overmanaged, or simply poorly managed. These cases are more than likely the result of the "Peter Principle." Few managers of Christian organizations have had sound training in management theory and practice. They moved into their management positions because they were recognized as being more effective than others in what they were already doing. They may not fear management as being unspiritual, but they may fear failure through not managing at all. Consequently, these managers compensate for their inexperience by investing heavily in all of the latest management trends, without really understanding the function of management in an organization.

Whatever the reason, sloppy, inadequate, or inefficient management of Christian organizations compromises the ethical integrity of the organization because it defrauds those who have invested in the organization as well as those who are the intended recipients of the work of the organization. Why is this fraud? Because poor management squanders the resources invested in the organization. These resources represent the investment of human lives. Christian organizations thus do wrong to their neighbors through inefficient and inadequate managing of the organization.

When Paul said "we aim at what is honorable not only in the Lord's sight but also in the sight of men," he was thinking of the ethical integrity that belongs to the excellence of love. It is a mark of effective leadership to be able to lead and inspire the management of Christian organizations to this high level of ethical integrity.

The excellence of Christian organizations in this area can be directly attributed to the effectiveness of its leadership in implementing the mandate of love—do no wrong to your neighbor.

EXCELLENCE AS HUMAN ECOLOGY

A second mark of excellence in Christian organizations is focused more directly upon the quality of life experienced by those who are part of the organization. Love does no wrong to a neighbor. This means that love does not exploit others for its own gain.

"I will never work in a Christian organization again," a woman bitterly complained after leaving a large and well-known Christian college. "There is nothing Christian about the way they treat their employees—they exploit people in the name of Jesus." We have all heard similar complaints. Perhaps some are justified; perhaps some are not. Some may expect a Christian organization to be more like a local church, with no time clock and no expectations of work performance spelled out. Some people are greatly offended at the use of employee evaluation procedures on the part of Christian organizations. Some, like Lucy in the comic strip "Peanuts," feel that it is sufficient to excuse not catching a fly ball hit to the outfield by saying, "I was having my devotions."

But I suspect that in far too many cases, Christian organizations have thoughtlessly exploited their staff by assuming that low pay, inadequate benefits, and sacrifices for the sake of the organization all belong to that which is distinctive about Christian organizations—all is done to the glory of God. After all, they may be told, their real "payday" is when the Lord will say, "Well done, good and faithful servant."

Love does no wrong to a neighbor. Rather, love seeks the good of the neighbor. A mark of excellence in Christian organizations is certainly what we might call the "human ecology" of the organization in terms of how employees and staff are treated.

Sacrifice is one of the privileges, if not the calling, of Christians for the sake of Christ. The apostle Paul gloried in the sacrifices that he made for the sake of the gospel. But a true sacrifice for the sake of Christ is itself a gift that a person makes, and that results in a dignity and value of the person that is not often achieved in any other way.

Exploitation of the sacrifice of others, however, is doing wrong to a neighbor. Exploitation occurs when one person gains through the sacrifice of another, or when the organization itself, as an impersonal and institutional structure, gains by the sacrifice of those who contribute their own personal and spiritual lives and resources.

Christian organizations are very susceptible to the danger of exploitation because they are often in a position to manipulate the sacrificial faith of Christians for the objectives of the organization. This is why the leadership of Christian organizations must be especially scrupulous in this area.

When managers in Christian organizations compete in the job market for employees, they have an "edge" that they can often use. "I need a good paying job to support my two children," a woman said to me recently, "but I also want to work in a Christian organization, so I realize that I will have to make some sacrifices." The woman's resume indicated that she had indeed held jobs that paid more than a commensurate job would pay in this particular Christian organization. The temptation was to offer her the lower pay, with the assurance that I had "an edge" in terms of hiring her.

One could argue that God is glorified by achieving our production goals at lower cost and greater efficiency because Christians will work at lower pay for the privilege of working with other Christians. Managers thus have an "edge" when it comes to balancing the budget and satisfying the trustees, who look for sound fiscal management as a sign of good leadership in a Christian organization. The doxology is sung in the annual meeting of the board of trustees because another year was finished "in the black." But the woman and her two children are not there to join in the praise to God.

We need to listen to Paul again. "Open your hearts to us; we have wronged no one, we have corrupted no one, we have taken advantage of no one," he wrote to the Corinthians (2 Cor. 7:2). Paul reminded the Christians at Corinth that his ministry among them was not on the same terms as those "false apostles" who entered in to take advantage of them (2 Cor. 11:12-13).

To the Thessalonian Christians he wrote:

> For we never used either words of flattery, as you know, or a cloak for greed, as God is witness. . . . So, being affectionately desirous of you, we were ready to share with you not only the gospel of God but also our own selves, because you had become very dear to us. (1 Thess. 2:5, 8)

Paul practiced what I have called "human ecology" as part of his ministry of the gospel. He saw neither his converts nor his fellow workers as impersonal means to an end, but rather as part of the end, part of the goal. He was as careful to conserve and sustain the personal and human lives of people as he was faithful to witness to the gospel of Christ with all effectiveness.

Leadership must care as much about what is given to people as about what is taken from them. For Christ is not glorified in what he accomplishes through using people to serve his own ends, but rather is glorified in the conserving and building up of those who are given to him. This is strikingly evident in his so-called high priestly prayer recorded in John 17. Jesus first makes clear that he is concerned for the "human ecology" of those whom the Father has given him. He has manifested the

Father's name to them (v. 6); he has given them the words the Father had given to him (v. 8); he is praying for them (v. 9); and he is "glorified in them" (v. 10). He then tells the Father that he has kept them "in thy name"; "I have guarded them, and none of them is lost but the son of perdition" (v. 12). Finally, he asks the Father to "sanctify them in the truth," and then says that "for their sake I consecrate myself, that they also may be consecrated in truth" (vv. 17, 19).

Here is surely the model for the practice of "human ecology" in the managing of Christian organizations! A mark of excellence in Christian organizations must be the consecration of those who work in the organization through the consecration of the leadership to the task of leading others to glorify Christ.

The woman who bitterly complained to me about having been exploited in a Christian organization ultimately did not leave because of the inadequate pay scale, nor was she complaining about this factor. She knew what she was doing when she accepted the job. No one compelled her to work in that particular place. No, her complaint was that she was exploited, because what was to have been a meaningful sacrifice on her part was credited to the account of those who managed the organization. She felt "used" in the sense that her own work was taken for granted while others took credit for its value. She did not have managers like the apostle Paul, who could "share with her their own lives." Rather, she found an absence of Christian love as translated into recognition of her as a person and as the giving back to her in kind of some of the personal and spiritual life that she was devoting to the institution.

I suppose some would say that if this woman really was doing her job for the Lord, then the Lord should be sufficient for her. If that is the case, why did Paul give of himself in such a costly way to the churches he managed and to his own fellow workers?

No, there is a human ecology that has its roots in the incarnation of God himself. This is the mark of God's excellence, that he did not merely demand sacrifice, but that he gave of himself, and sacrificed himself for his neighbors.

Effective leadership will practice this same human ecology as a mark of excellence in Christian organizations. It can be done without compromising sound business and management practices. In fact, as Peters and Waterman found, those companies which had the marks of excellence were also those which practiced this human ecology, in one form or another. We know that this is more than a pragmatic form of good management—it is the work of love.

EXCELLENCE AS PERSONAL ADVOCACY

A friend and colleague in a Christian organization once confided in me, "I feel very vulnerable in this organization. I feel that no one really is my advocate. I am paid adequately, and I enjoy working here. But I have the feeling that decisions could be made about my work or my future with no one really on my side." Love, however, does no wrong to a neighbor—it does not fail others in their time of need. A third mark of excellence in Christian organizations is personal advocacy.

Advocacy is a further aspect of the practice of human ecology. What makes it a mark of excellence in its own right is the fact that it springs into action especially when an individual, or a segment of the organization, is threatened by actions over which it has no control. An organization has its strongest instincts tuned for its own survival. Management is by itself an impersonal process, a method or technique of enabling the organization to achieve its purpose and goals. Human ecology can be practiced as a continuing effort to uphold and sustain the value of persons who function in the organization. But advocacy is a quality of leadership whose absence is only noted when there is a critical need for it.

When asked to take on an additional administrative assignment that involved supervision of a program unit in a Christian organization, I replied, "I will, but only with the understanding that I will become an advocate for the program in discussions that affect its destiny." My conviction was that leadership involved advocacy, and that a person who directs a program should also be the strongest advocate for the program. This advocacy, of course, must be exercised within the overall decision-making process of the organization. Advocacy is not a stubborn defense of what is indefensible; it is a distribution of power from the strong to the weak.

"We who are strong," wrote Paul, "ought to bear with the failings of the weak, and not to please ourselves; let each of us please his neighbor for his good, to edify him" (Rom. 15:1-2). Paul then went on to cite the example of Christ who "did not please himself; but, as it is written, 'The reproaches of those who reproached thee fell on me'" (v. 3). This is personal advocacy. It is the love of the neighbor carried out when the neighbor is in a weak position—and love will not fail one in time of need.

One of the most powerful examples of leadership and the exercise of personal advocacy is that of Moses. When he descended from Mt. Sinai with the tablets of the law in his hands, he was confronted by the apostasy and idolatry of Israel as the people worshiped the golden calf (Exod. 32). God's judgment was that they should be destroyed, and that he would make out of Moses a great nation. Moses, however, became the advocate on behalf of the people, and rejected the offer to become, himself, the founder of a new nation. He interceded before God for the people, and shifted the power from his own strategic position with God to the people in their own vulnerability and need. "Alas," Moses said to God, "this people have sinned a great sin; they have made for themselves gods of gold. But now, if thou wilt forgive their sin—and if not, blot me, I pray thee, out of thy book which thou has written" (32:31-32).

Advocacy assumes that there is a power that can be invested on behalf of others in their own situation of powerlessness. Otherwise, advocacy would only be sympathy. Advocacy is, therefore, an attribute of leadership, for only leadership has access to this power. The failure of leadership to exercise advocacy on behalf of those in need within the organization abandons the weak to their own fate.

It is not for nothing that Jesus told his disciples, "I will pray the Father, and he will give you another counselor, to be with you for ever" (John 14:16). Jesus, it is clear, considers himself to be the first advocate, or *paraclete;* the Holy Spirit will be another advocate sent to carry out the advocacy of Jesus himself.

One remembers how strongly Jesus expressed himself when he likened those who were great in the kingdom of heaven to a little child, and then said, "Whoever receives one such child receives me; but whoever causes one of these little ones who believe in me to sin, it would be better for him to have a great millstone fastened round his neck and to be drowned in the depth of the sea" (Matt. 18:5-6). Scholars suggest that "these little ones" refers to Jesus' own disciples, not merely to children. For whatever happened, the disciples surely knew that Jesus would be "on their side," so to speak, and would throw his strength alongside of their weakness.

Management tends to "go by the book" in dealing with personnel matters, even in Christian organizations. This is well and good, as a basis for establishing policy. There is no policy manual for effective leadership, however. That is why personal advocacy is a mark of effective leadership, in addition to efficient management technique.

There is another side to advocacy that may be missed. Advocacy is not a blind and stubborn defense of that which is indefensible. It is an intervention into a human and personal situation that is about to become the victim of an inhuman and impersonal process of organizational bureaucracy. In this act of intervention, there is both advocacy and discipline. For example, Moses did not deny that the people had sinned. His advocacy was not for the purpose of excusing their sin, but for preserving their relationship with God. It was his advocacy for the people that gave Moses the authority to discipline them. And discipline them he did!

There is a lesson to be learned here. Discipline that is not based on advocacy will in most cases be counterproductive. Only those who have first of all shown the leadership of advocacy will be effective in correcting abuses and disciplining the organization. Discipline is only effective where there has been a transfer of power from the strong to the weak. This transfer of power reinforces the personal and spiritual life of the person who needs either to make improvement or to change. Only when this transfer of power has taken place will the authority of leadership be effective as a disciplinary function.

This, again, is modeled by Jesus. In dealing with the woman caught in adultery, he first of all became her personal advocate over and against the impersonal demands of the law. Technically, by the book, she was guilty and deserved to be stoned. Instead, Jesus effected a transfer of power by standing with her against her accusers. With her humanity and dignity as a person restored, Jesus then asked, "'Has no one condemned you?' She said, 'No one, Lord.' And Jesus said, 'Neither do I condemn you; go, and do not sin again'" (John 8:1-11).

Effective leadership in personal advocacy requires the sensitivity and courage that love brings into a Christian organization. Those who give leadership to Christian organizations are probably sending signals quite unobtrusively as to whether or not they will offer personal advocacy. My friend and colleague had received no positive signals that he would have an advocate to represent him when he needed it the most. He feels increasingly powerless. I suspect that he will become anxious and even angry. Then his loyalty and productivity will be questioned, and when he leaves or his position is terminated, it will be as another casualty of Christian organizations.

Love does no wrong to a neighbor—it does not fail in time of need. This is why personal advocacy is a mark of excellence.

EXCELLENCE AS SPIRITUAL PARITY

The marks of excellence we are exploring all issue out of the commandment of love. For divine love is the excellence of God as exhibited through Jesus Christ. In applying this commandment, Paul said, "Love does no wrong to a neighbor; therefore, love is the fulfilling of the law" (Rom. 13:10). In this regard, it is wrong to deprive others of their full share in the enterprise that constitutes the life and purpose of a Christian organization. A mark of excellence, therefore, is spiritual parity on the part of all members of the organization.

The laborer deserves his wages, as Jesus taught (Luke 10:7). Paul wrote to Timothy, "Let the elders who rule well be considered worthy of double honor, especially those who labor in preaching and teaching" (1 Tim. 5:17). And then he added the very words Jesus cited: "The laborer deserves his wages."

The matter of what constitutes fair and sufficient compensation is a point we cannot enter into here. What does concern us is the assumption that equality of compensation, by whatever form it is given, is the principle that should govern the policies of Christian organizations.

What is of concern, I believe, is what I would prefer to call parity, rather than equality. In our day, equality tends to be defined in terms of that which is exactly the same, whether it be roles, privileges, or compensation. Behind this lurks the ideological issue of "rights" and the assumption that an equal share in power is the only way to balance the struggle for power. Spiritual parity, however, does not mean equality in role, rank, and salary compensation. Some Christian organizations attempt to base the distinctive characteristic of the organization on a flat pay scale for all employees, adjusted only in increments related to family size and cost of living factors. This is unrealistic and, in a certain sense, unfair.

A family, on the other hand, operates on the basis that the role functions are not all identical, nor are the privileges and compensations exactly the same for parents as for children. What is of concern is that each member of the family have a *full share* in the enterprise represented by the family. This full share is what is meant by having parity.

A Christian organization is an enterprise, somewhat similar to a family, but also somewhat different. It is similar in that it represents a community of persons whose common cause is related to the fulfillment of a task for the glory of God in Jesus Christ. While not a community of persons in exactly the same way that a local church is, it nonetheless is one manifestation of that same community as defined by the particular purpose of the organization.

By saying that excellence in Christian organizations is marked by spiritual parity, I do not mean to suggest that one should expect that spiritual rewards are sufficient compensation, so that material compensation is unnecessary, or at best a "necessary evil." No. Spiritual parity is grounded in what we have called human ecology. Human persons invest their energies, time, and spirit in their work as a part of Christian organizations. Spiritual parity is a full share in the "spirit" of the organization as a community of Christians involved in the common cause expressed by the mission statement of the organization.

One obvious manifestation of this "spirit" is the recognition and response of others to what the organization accomplishes. This recognition and response is what was sought by the hypocrites who disfigured their faces so that they might be seen by men (Matt. 6:16); by the rich who offer large sums of money publicly, in contrast to the poor widow, who gave her "two mites," which was all that she had (Mark 12:41-42). Those who perform for the applause and recognition of others "have their reward," said Jesus. But he did not deny that there is a reward for which all should seek. And that reward is the personal recognition that comes from God. This reward does not encourage hypocrisy and is not gained at the expense of others. Rather, this reward gives full share in the fruit of love. As Christians who give leadership in Christian organizations, we dispense this full share in the fruit of love as recognition and compensation for the investment of the lives of others in the purpose and goal of the organization.

"Every person seeks meaning," Peters and Waterman have told us. This meaning is compensation for the expenditure of one's life energies, including time, work, and material resources. Because human life is essentially a spiritual and not a materialist, functional existence, one expects and needs a full share in what life offers by way of fulfillment of this need.

"He who receives a prophet because he is a prophet shall receive a prophet's reward," taught Jesus.

And he who receives a righteous man because he is a righteous man shall receive a righteous man's reward. And whoever gives to one of these little ones even a cup of cold water because he is a disciple, truly, I say to you, he shall not lose his reward. (Matt. 10:41-42)

Spiritual parity is one way of speaking of the fact that each member of the Christian organization can receive a full share in the "reward" that comes from faithful service to Christ in the organization.

Those who exercise leadership are custodians of the rewards a Christian organization administers on behalf of Jesus. If these rewards are measured solely in terms of perks for executives, bonuses for outstanding performers, or assigned parking spaces for favored employees, wrong will be done to the neighbor. Instead, it is the privilege and responsibility of the leadership of Christian organizations to give full parity to each member of the organization; that is, to see that no employee is unrewarded for the full expenditure of faith, time, and energy that he or she gives to the organization.

How is this done? How do parents insure that children have full parity? Not by heaping presents upon them, but by including them in the rituals and celebrations of the life of the family. Parity means sharing in the equivalence of love that is given and received through the daily transactions of family life. Manuals on management do not ordinarily teach techniques for giving parity in this way. One notable exception to this is the currently popular little book written by Kenneth Blanchard and Spencer Johnson, *The One Minute Manager,* which is based on one form of this simple axiom—pay attention to people, and give strokes at the appropriate time.[6] It pays off in the end!

What we have suggested by way of these marks of excellence only begins to stretch the imagination as to how effective leadership can maintain quality control for Christian organizations. Our thesis has been that the character of a Christian organization is rooted in its quality of life as measured by the love of God in Christ displayed in the basic human and personal relations that constitute the daily life of the organization as a community. We have attempted to make a case for excellence in Christian organizations through an exposition of the commandment of love as the touchstone of excellence.

Christian organizations, in addition to making a statement of beliefs as a confession of what they are, and in addition to making a statement of mission as a confession of what they are about, also are making a statement about the character of Jesus Christ in their quality of life. This, finally, may be the most effective confession and testimony that the world will see.

Christian organization—do right by your neighbor!

6. K. Blanchard and S. Johnson, *The One Minute Manager* (New York: Morrow, 1982).

CHAPTER SEVEN

BUT IS ALL OF THIS REALLY SPIRITUAL?

"The Lord is the manager of this organization, and we don't take one step without being directed by the Holy Spirit and bathing each project in prayer."

The man who said this to me was head of a quite successful Christian organization. The context of his statement was our discussion of the use of management principles and techniques for Christian organizations.

He was frankly suspicious.

"I have seen too many organizations begin with the Spirit, and end with the flesh," he went on, warming up to the subject. "What once was a work of God, in total reliance upon him, can become a work of man, using secular means and methods. God is not honored by that."

I had to listen, as he went on to remind me of what the Scriptures teach.

The Tower of Babel invited the judgment of God precisely because it appeared to be an engineering success (Gen. 11:1-9). Israel was always tempted to import the technology of other nations as a more effective means of making war and preserving its own peace. "Woe to those who go down to Egypt for help and rely on horses, who trust in chariots because they are many and in horsemen because they are very strong," cried out Isaiah (31:1). "Not by might, nor by power, but by my Spirit, says the Lord of hosts," was the message Zechariah presented to the people to encourage them in the rebuilding of the temple following the exile (Zech. 4:6).

I remembered that the apostle warned the church that it would be engaged in a *spiritual* warfare, and that its weapons for this battle were to be spiritual. Consequently, Paul wrote, "Be strong in the Lord and in the strength of his might. Put on the whole armor of God. . . . Take the helmet of salvation and the sword of the Spirit, which is the word of God. Pray at all times in the Spirit" (Eph. 6:10-11, 17-18).

In light of this, we should ask ourselves, Is all of this talk about management for Christian organizations really spiritual? What is the place of the Holy Spirit in the planning process? Is prayer a more effective means of accomplishing our goals than reliance upon human means and methods? Does not the providence of God mean that he will bless that which is committed to him so that it cannot fail? If it is God's business, is he not finally accountable for its success, and we only for obedience and faithfulness?

Let us admit that these questions have been in our mind from the beginning. We wondered at the outset whether it is God who does the planning and managing and we the work, or whether we do the planning and managing and God does the work. We never did answer that question because it assumes a dichotomy between planning and work that we do not find in God himself. Nor do we agree that such a dichotomy can be made between God's work and our work. Nor, for that matter, can there ever be a clear separation between our business and God's business.

The questions we are now asking, however, are legitimate ones, and demand some answers. The role of the Holy Spirit in minding God's business as well as the practical place of prayer are of vital concern to us. We must also reckon with the fact that the providence of God is at work through our planning and is to be made manifest in our work. Thus, let us take up these issues one at a time.

THE HOLY SPIRIT AND MANAGING
CHRISTIAN ORGANIZATIONS

Some have suggested that a more appropriate title for the New Testament book entitled The Acts of the Apostles would be The Acts of the Holy Spirit. Following his resurrection, Jesus warns his disciples that they should not depart from Jerusalem until the promise comes upon them from the Father, and they are "baptized with the Holy Spirit" (Acts 1:4-5). Before his ascension, Jesus promised the disciples, "You shall receive power when the Holy Spirit has come upon you; and you shall be my witnesses in Jerusalem and in all Judea and Samaria and to the end of the earth" (Acts 1:8).

The promise of the Holy Spirit is coupled with the setting forth of an action plan, with quite specific instruction as to its procedure and purpose. The disciples are first of all to wait and to be equipped. Then they are to begin in Jerusalem and Judea and, working through Samaria, to continue to the "ends of the earth." Following Pentecost, the disciples did indeed begin to follow out this plan as led and empowered by the Spirit. Being filled with the Holy Spirit was a rather common way to speak of the experience of Christ's resurrection power at work through their own testimony and ministry (see Acts 4:8-10).

In the church at Antioch, Luke tells us, while the Christians were worshiping the Lord and fasting, "the Holy Spirit said, 'Set apart for me Barnabas and Saul for the work to which I have called them'" (Acts 13:2). We are not told how this word came from the Holy Spirit, but it is clear that the church did not question that their decisions, intentions, and plans were directed by the Spirit of Jesus himself.

Somewhat later, when a church council had to make a strategic decision with regard to the relation between the Gentile churches founded by Paul and the church in Jerusalem, the apostles and elders came to a decision that they announced in this interesting fashion: "It has seemed good to us, having come to one accord, to choose men and send them to you. . . . For it has seemed good to the Holy Spirit and to us to lay upon you no greater burden than these necessary things" (Acts 15:25, 28).

There appears to be a clue for us here as to the manner in which the early church determined that its actions were also the direct leading of the Holy Spirit. In the first instance (chap. 13), it is in the context of the gathered and worshiping church that the people "hear" the Holy Spirit speak instructions to them concerning Barnabas and Saul. Luke does not disclose their own deliberations and discussion of the various options; nor does he disclose what means they took to confirm that it was indeed the leading of the Holy Spirit to take this strategic action.

In the second instance (chap. 15), we are told a great deal more about the nature of the discussion and are even told that the action to be taken came out of a consensus reached through that discussion. James, in acting as the spokesperson for the council, explains that the decision seemed good both "to the Holy Spirit and to us." Here we see that the leading of the Holy Spirit does not provide a "short cut" to decisions and action plans; rather, the Holy Spirit works along with this human process. Again, what Luke presents to us is a picture of the church working toward consensus, both as to the action plan as well as to the leading of the Holy Spirit.

This consensus is not always easily attained. Luke tells us that at the end of what we know as his third missionary journey, Paul "resolved in the Spirit to pass through Macedonia and Achaia and go to Jerusalem, saying, 'After I have been there, I must also see Rome'" (Acts 19:21). After making his journey to Macedonia and Achaia, Paul makes a farewell speech to the elders from the church at Ephesus in which he says, "I am going to Jerusalem, bound in the Spirit, not knowing what shall befall me there; except that the Holy Spirit testifies to me in every city that imprisonment and afflictions await me" (Acts 20:22-23).

It is quite clear that Paul himself is convinced that his personal plans are grounded in the leading of the Spirit, even though he is also made aware of the fact that this will entail much difficulty. What is also clear is that, having "resolved in the Spirit" to go, and "being bound in the Spirit," Paul still does not have advance details as to how the venture will work out. For he admits that he does not know "what shall befall me there." However, when Paul arrived at Tyre, the Christian disciples, "through the Spirit," tell him not to go on to Jerusalem (Acts 21:4). Yet he and his company continued on their journey, apparently with the good will of those same disciples, even though Paul did not heed their warning, delivered "through the Spirit."

Upon his arrival in Caesarea, Paul entered the house of Philip the evangelist, where he was visited by Agabus, a prophet from Jerusalem, who, taking Paul's own girdle, bound his hands and feet saying, "Thus says the Holy Spirit, 'So shall the Jews at Jerusalem bind the man who owns this girdle and deliver him into the hands of the Gentiles'" (Acts 21:11). Luke writes, "When we heard this, we and the people there begged him not to go to Jerusalem." Yet Paul would not be dissuaded from his plan, and Luke adds, "When he would not be persuaded, we ceased and said, 'The will of the Lord be done'" (Acts 21:14).

We have followed Luke's account of this scenario in Paul's life and ministry in order to demonstrate the point that the role of the Holy Spirit in the determination of plans is a very complex and subtle relationship between the factors of expediency, common sense, human will, group dynamics, and prophetic utterance. In the end, when Paul's friends and companions saw that he could not be persuaded, they surrendered their own claims to a private spiritual leading from the Holy Spirit to the purpose of the Holy Spirit in working out the will of the Lord in Paul's life.

This is a very important and instructive lesson for us. The Holy Spirit is, in fact, the same Spirit of the risen Lord Jesus who works with and through his people to accomplish his will. The leading of the Holy Spirit in a situation is not independent of the will of the Lord through the situation.

In Chapter Five, we saw how the will of God is embodied in the goal as the outworking of promise, rather than in a specific set of action plans or decisions. Now we see how important this is. For the role of the Holy Spirit in the management of Christian organizations is not to bring his own plans or to exert his own will, but to empower those in whom the Spirit dwells to fulfill the will of the Lord through their own lives and actions.

Paul does not seem to be concerned that the messages he receives through others as coming from the Holy Spirit may contradict his own commitment to do the will of the Lord. Nor are the others concerned to hold to their assurance that they have the mind of the Spirit against Paul's own intentions. They, as well as Paul, seem to know instinctively that the Holy Spirit is not the "missing piece" of the puzzle, so that whoever has this "piece" has the answer to some secret plan that originates in the mind of God.

No, the Holy Spirit is not the missing link in our management techniques and action plans. He is the enabling power of Christ himself working with and through our struggles to do what is right as well as most effective, so that in the end, Christ is glorified.

We can summarize what we understand to be the role of the Holy Spirit in managing Christian organizations as follows:

1. We are to understand the Holy Spirit to be the Spirit of the Lord Jesus, directing, empowering, and equipping Christians to accomplish his will.

2. The Holy Spirit is not a substitute for planning, nor is he the "missing piece" in a puzzle by which God's secret plan is made known.

3. Openness to the leading of the Holy Spirit safeguards human plans and decisions from the error of confusing the will of God with any one decision or plan. Plans are the human means for achieving goals that embody the promise of God and complete the will of God.

4. The spiritual aspect of managing Christian organizations is not itself the use of a spiritual method or means as against any other method. Rather, the spiritual dimension of managing is represented by bringing all of the methods and means used into the service of the spiritual goal—that of achieving the will of the Lord and glorifying him in the process.

5. One important role of the Holy Spirit in the managing of Christian organizations, then, is to invest the reality and freedom of Christ as a living presence and power in the dynamic process of leading an organization to set goals, establish priorities, create action plans, and work with all contingencies that occur.

6. The Holy Spirit gives to an organization a creative response to contingencies, so that the "unforeseen" can be enfolded into the planning process without undercutting the validity of the plan. The Holy Spirit lends courage and resourcefulness to those who make and execute action plans. Working in tandem with the planning and decision-making process, the Spirit is not discouraged by opposing insights and convictions, nor is he committed to one view as opposed to another. But the concern of the Spirit is that "the will of the Lord be done."

"It seemed good to the Holy Spirit and to us." Those who provide leadership for Christian organizations must be competent in providing this kind of "spiritual" leadership. For it is "not by might, nor by power, but by my Spirit, says the Lord of hosts" (Zech. 4:6).

PRAYER AND MANAGING CHRISTIAN ORGANIZATIONS

I referred earlier in this book to the method used by George Mueller of Bristol, England, in raising support for the orphanages he established. Refusing to rely upon any sort of public appeal for funds, he brought his needs directly to God in prayer, and his testimony was that God supplied all of his needs through earnest and faithful prayer. What pastor or leader of a Christian organization has not suffered an uneasy conscience over this issue?

The promise of Jesus appears so direct and simple: "Whatever you ask in prayer, you will receive, if you have faith" (Matt. 21:22); "Ask, and it will be given you; seek, and you will find; knock, and it will be opened to you" (Matt. 7:7).

"You do not have, because you do not ask. You ask and do not receive, because you ask wrongly, to spend it on your passions," scolds James (4:3).

Tell that to the apostle Paul! When he was troubled by a "thorn in the flesh" that obviously hindered his ministry (he thought), he wrote: "Three times I besought the Lord about this, that it should leave me; but he said to me, 'My grace is sufficient for you, for my power is made perfect in weakness'" (2 Cor. 12:8-9).

True, Paul did receive grace sufficient to live with his affliction, but George Mueller received food for hungry children, not a double portion of patience and grace to live without what he asked for!

Surely our wisdom concerning prayer is the least of our wisdom as Christians. And yet, it is precisely the issue of prayer that often has the power to tie us up in spiritual knots and leave us with the paralyzing fear that this may be our greatest failure.

What place does prayer have in managing Christian organizations? Is prayer the "spiritual" work that sanctifies the otherwise unspiritual and secular side of "minding God's business"? Does my friend, quoted at the outset of this chapter, have the spiritual edge when he says, "We don't take one step without being directed by the Holy Spirit, and bathing each project in prayer"? Does this mean that every step taken by his organization and every project it creates succeeds rather than fails? I am afraid to ask.

I am not afraid to ask the apostle, however. We remember that Paul has set forth for Jerusalem via Macedonia and Achaia as the first leg of his planned journey to Rome and then on to Spain. A rather ambitious plan! No wonder that he fortified himself by "resolving in the Spirit" and continuing to press forward in the plan despite opposition of a highly "spiritual" nature, by letting it be known that he was "bound in the Spirit" (Acts 19:21; 20:22).

Before he set out on this venture, however, he sat down in Ephesus and wrote a letter to the church in Rome advising them of his intentions and seeking to enlist their support in the further mission to Spain. Near the end of this letter, he asked the Christians in Rome to pray for him:

> I appeal to you, brethren, by our Lord Jesus Christ and by the love of the Spirit, to strive together with me in your prayers to God on my behalf, that I may be delivered from the unbelievers in Judea, and that my service for Jerusalem may be acceptable to the saints, so that by God's will I may come to you with joy and be refreshed in your company. (Rom. 15:30-32)

This prayer is quite specific, and there is no reason to think that the Christians in Rome did not pray exactly as Paul asked them to pray.

What are we to think, then, when we discover that when Paul arrived in Jerusalem he was arrested within a few days and charged with undermining the Jewish law and customs? He then spent two years languishing in prison at Caesarea, due to the insistent pressure put upon Felix by the Jews from Jerusalem and the political ambivalence of Felix himself. Not only that, forced to appeal to Caesar to escape this bad situation, he barely survived a treacherous winter sea journey, being shipwrecked on the island of Malta, and ended up in Rome in chains, where he spent at least another two years in prison!

The point of the whole plan, of course, was to get to Spain to preach the gospel; but there is no clue in Scripture as to whether he ever did accomplish this goal, assuming that he was released from prison in Rome eventually.

Yet, writing to the church in Philippi from prison (assumably in Rome), Paul can say: "I want you to know, brethren, that what has happened to me has really served to advance the gospel" (Phil. 1:12).

Let us see what Paul's experience can teach us about the role of prayer in managing Christian organizations.

First, we must see that prayer is not a means of making plans "fail-safe," at least in terms of some kind of direct cause-and-effect relation such that prayer is the cause and the working of a plan the effect. This concept of cause and effect, when attached to prayer, turns prayer into magic and reduces God to an impersonal force attached to a "prayer wheel."

Second, we discover that prayer actually delivers the plans we make from the spiritual devastation of a "success/failure" syndrome. Paul's real goal is to glorify Christ—his plans were only a means to that end. This was, in fact, his answer to those who sought to change his plans through the "spiritual leverage" of the Holy Spirit, if I may be permitted to say so in order to make a point.

"What are you doing, weeping and breaking my heart?" cries out Paul. "For I am ready not only to be imprisoned but even to die at Jerusalem for the name of the Lord Jesus" (Acts 21:13). When they heard him say this, his friends conceded, and said, "The will of the Lord be done."

If you were to ask Paul if his plans were successful, he would probably say that they worked well enough in light of the fact that his ultimate goal was reached—to glorify Christ through his life. Thus, his prayers, and those of the Christians in Rome, were effective precisely because they were attached to his plans for the sake of his goal to glorify Jesus Christ, whether by life or death. It was not as though the plans were attached to the prayers in order to guarantee that the plans were to be successful as an end in themselves.

In other words, prayer that is not attached to action plans probably has little effect. For it is our plans that carry our prayers toward the ultimate goal of doing the will of God and glorifying Christ.

In his fine little book on prayer, Jacques Ellul has this to say about the relation of action to prayer:

Action really receives its character from prayer. Prayer is what attests the finitude of action and frees it from its dramatic or tragic aspect. Since it shows that the action is not final, it brings to it humor and reserve. Otherwise we would be tempted to take it with dreadful seriousness. But in so doing prayer bestows upon action its greatest authenticity. It rescues action from activism, and it rescues the individual from bewilderment and despair in his action. It prevents his being engulfed in panic when his action fails, and from being drawn into activism, when he is incited to more and more activity in pursuit of success, to the point of losing himself. Prayer, because it is the warrant, the expression of my finitude, always teaches me that I must *be more* than my action, that I must live with my action, and even that my action must be lived with by another in *his* action. Thanks to prayer, I can see that truth about myself and my action, in hope and not in despair.[1]

I have quoted Ellul at length because he seems to describe so accurately the way in which Paul viewed prayer with respect to his own action plans. "Prayer," says Ellul, "is flexibility within organizational rigidity."[2] This is true. Organizational life tends to become rigid precisely because it tends to operate on the cause-and-effect principle. Prayer opens up the life of the organization to an aim on the goal that includes plans and methods but does not invest in plans and methods the fate of the organization.

There is a third lesson that we learn from our meditation upon Paul's experience. Prayer precedes action plans rather than being the spiritual factor attached to plans. All too often the sequence is that of agreeing to spontaneous action, or even of reaching consensus concerning deliberate action and then adding prayer as a means of insuring that the plan or project will succeed. This lies behind the language used by my friend—every project is bathed in prayer. So it should be, if it has itself emerged out of prayer!

It is from prayer that action derives its character and values. For it is in and through prayer that the ultimate goal of individual and organizational action takes form. It is through prayer that one focuses clearly on the true goal, that of seeking to do the will of God and to glorify Jesus Christ, whether in life or death.

1. J. Ellul, *Prayer and Modern Man* (New York: Seabury, 1973), p. 172.
2. Ibid., p. 175.

Such an understanding of prayer releases us from the spiritual bondage that often results from an attempt to understand prayer as a spiritual means to a successful end of a plan or decision. It also frees us from making preposterous statements concerning the effectiveness of prayer in guaranteeing results.

Does prayer have a place in managing Christian organizations? It certainly does if one wishes to avoid the despair and to be liberated from the hypocrisy that come from using prayer to guarantee that every decision and every project can succeed. Prayer heals managers of this dreadful disease, and liberates organizations to find ways to glorify Christ through effective service.

PROVIDENCE AND MANAGING CHRISTIAN ORGANIZATIONS

The deeper issue hidden behind the use of prayer and the leading of the Holy Spirit as spiritual means to insure success in our endeavors is the feeling that God, in his sovereignty, controls all things from the beginning to the end. This sovereign will of God is often understood as predetermining events and history to conform to his eternal will and purpose. From this perspective it is divine providence that insures that a venture succeeds, provided, of course, that we are spiritually attuned to God's will and plan.

We often hear people say of someone else's ministry, "The hand of God is surely on his life"; or, "God has blessed that organization in an unusual way." And so we ought to say, for God does bestow his blessings upon his children, and his hand indeed is strong to work wonders through those who are his servants.

The Bible is quite clear that God is the sovereign Lord of all creation, and that he does exercise his power to effect his will through all events. The word of God to Job, in the end, made it quite clear as to who was in control! And Jesus reassured his followers that as the Father cares for the birds of the air and the lilies of the field, so he will also care for us so that we need not be anxious (Matt. 6:25-33). God's sovereign knowledge

includes the "sparrow that falls to the ground"; "even the hairs
of your head are numbered," said Jesus (Matt. 10:29-30).

We do not for one minute question the sovereignty of God
in terms of his knowledge and will. Nor do we doubt that he
causes events to work toward his purpose, so that there is a
providence of God in which we can hope and trust. So the
apostle Paul was able to say: "We know that in everything God
works for good with those who love him, who are called according to his purpose" (Rom. 8:28). And thus he is led to ask,
"If God is for us, who is against us?" (8:31).

But all of this is not quite the same as saying that the sovereignty of God is also like a blueprint, or plan, that exists first
of all in the mind of God and then must be determined
through some spiritual means or insight. Nor does God's sovereignty mean that he does not operate with freedom within
events in order to accomplish his purpose. In this way, God's
sovereignty does not preclude human freedom, but actually
frees human action and decisions from fatalism and despair.

We have already seen how Paul understands the providence
of God with respect to his own plans. He does not use prayer
and a subjective dependence upon the leading of the Holy
spirit to "read God's mind," so to speak. Nor does he act as
though the success or failure of his own plans confirms in
some way the providence of God. Rather, for Paul the providence of God is God's promise and his freedom to work
through the events in Paul's life to accomplish his purpose.

Let me put it this way. The providence of God is not God's
"strategic plan" that is the "final cause" behind our own history and plans. The purpose of prayer and the leading of the
Holy Spirit are not to insure that our plans and actions are to
be directly identified with God's sovereign will. On the contrary, it is through prayer and dependence upon the Holy
Spirit that our plans are delivered from this "fateful" destiny
and left within the freedom of our own history and responsibility to be worked out.

Consider this scenario, for example. A Christian organization has in its mission statement the goal of distributing Christian literature to unevangelized tribes in South America as a
means of presenting the gospel of Jesus Christ. In attempting
to carry out this goal, obstacles arise that become insurmount-
able: there are problems with having the literature translated

into the various tribal languages, and few of the people for which the literature is prepared are literate. A consultant hired to assist in solving the problems suggests that the organization abandon attempts to communicate the gospel through literature and use radio communications instead. Not only do all of the people understand when spoken to in their own language, but inexpensive transistor radios locked on the frequency of the Christian broadcast can be produced and distributed much more efficiently than literature.

The administrative team of the Christian organization is in a quandary. Their mission statement commits the organization to the goal of distributing literature. In fact, the word *literature* is even part of their name! They have been operating on the assumption that their specific mission as identified by the goal of distributing literature was God's will for the organization.

In response to their quandary, the consultant told them of a company that had a successful business for many years manufacturing and selling electric drills. When they were edged out of the market through competitive products, they had to remember that their goal was not to manufacture electric drills, but to produce a product that would make holes! And they quickly made the shift to laser technology, which was more efficient.

What was involved for the Christian organization, however, was not only a technological shift, but a theological shift. Through theological reflection, the leadership of the Christian organization discovered that the promise of God is that his gospel shall be proclaimed and heard by all people. The use of literature was only a means to that end, and was not itself identical with the goal. It was through prayer and the leading of the Holy Spirit that the organization became liberated from the original plan to distribute literature, and moved freely and confidently into the field of radio communications. There is, in fact, no one-for-one identity between the goal and the method.

What had to take place, of course, was a revision of the mission statement of the organization so that the mission could be focused on the goal of communicating the gospel rather than on distributing literature. Thus, they avoided the "fate" of slowly becoming irrelevant due to an unworkable plan.

The providence of God is linked with the promise of God.

This is how the people of Israel understood the purpose of covenant. The covenant promise became the basis for understanding the sovereign power of God to effect his promise, in the face of all obstacles. We must never allow the providence of God to be detached from his promise and then linked with events themselves under the principle of causality. Our decisions and action plans are themselves part of what we call "events." Christian organizations create events through which the work of God can take place in order that God's promise may be realized.

Events do take place in the world that are neither planned nor the result of human decisions. Both natural disasters and unpredictable economic and political forces affect Christian organizations as well as secular organizations. When Jesus was asked why a man was born blind, he rejected the theory that it was "caused" by his parent's sin, as a sovereign judgment of God. Instead, he pointed to the work of God by which the man was healed as the "providence" of God (John 9).

Prayer and the leading of the Holy Spirit do not ordinarily manipulate events in the natural world in such a way that Christian organizations can be protected from casualty losses. Jesus taught that God "makes his sun rise on the evil and on the good, and sends rain on the just and on the unjust" (Matt. 5:45). If it should happen that God does supernaturally intervene in these events, then God is to be praised. But the Bible makes it quite clear that this is the extraordinary manifestation of his sovereignty in nature, and should in no case be the basis for a theology of providence by which nature or fate becomes the interpreter of God's providence.

Thus, Christian organizations, like any other organization, would do well to have a good medical plan for employees, insurance against catastrophic casualty loss of buildings and property, as well as a contingency plan in the event of an economic depression. Does this show lack of faith in God and a sign that the organization is no longer "spiritually minded"? Of course not.

Paul advised against setting sail from the port of Fair Havens on the leeward side of the Island of Crete due to the unpredictable winter storms. "Sirs," said Paul, addressing the captain and owner of the ship, "I perceive that the voyage will be with injury and much loss, not only of the cargo and the ship, but also of our lives" (Acts 27:10). It was not prayer and a direct leading of the Holy Spirit that lead Paul to give this good advice, but common sense. It was the captain and ship's owner who went ahead anyway on a foolhardy decision.

Many Christians, I am afraid, mistake foolhardiness for faith, and are suspicious of common sense, which they consider unspiritual. If managers of Christian organizations make this same mistake, there may well be a shipwreck. The astounding thing about God's providence, as those traveling with Paul discovered, is that it is not determined by events, either natural or caused by our own foolishness. Rather, God's providence is discovered as his sovereign upholding of his promise. It was the reaffirmation of the promise that gave Paul confidence in the midst of the storm, and led him to give good advice again, when the ship was breaking up on the rocks (Acts 27).

It is worth noting, however, that the providence of God that came to Paul in the form of a promise left room for certain contingencies. "I have faith in God," Paul told the captain of the ship, "that it will be exactly as I have been told." But then he added, "But we shall have to run on some island" (Acts 27:25-26). When they did indeed approach land, the sailors attempted to escape to safety by using the small shore boat. Seeing this, Paul immediately called out an alarm to the centurian and said, "Unless these men stay in the ship, you cannot be saved" (27:31). The next day, with the sailors aboard, they ran aground on a shoal, and all escaped. Paul's quick thinking and good planning were but part of how providence worked in order to accomplish the goal and realize the promise.

In a helpful discussion of the relation of divine providence to planning, the German theologian Jürgen Moltmann has this to say:

> The pious explanation of the providence of God in terms of an ultimate intention and plan was deistic through and through. "God" faded so that he became the mere decor of a plan which could be understood, to which history corresponded and would correspond. . . . The *novum* of God's promise becomes *fatum*.[3]

3. J. Moltmann, *Hope and Planning* (New York: Harper & Row, 1971), p. 187.

What Moltmann points out here is that providence, when viewed in terms of God's being the "final cause" of all events, reduces God's promise to a fate, rather than the new thing that works through history to accomplish his promise and purpose.

Planning and acting, says Moltmann, are not simply the reflection of an eternal will as the value, but are themselves "value-producing." In this sense, planning brings to bear the knowledge that is available from the past and present, and that "makes history." We can understand the providence of God, then, as God's freedom by which he "makes history" as the outworking of his providence.[4]

What does this mean for Christian organizations?

First, this understanding of providence means that the promise of God, revealed through his own actions in history, is for the good of human persons. This good is proclaimed as the gospel of Jesus Christ unto salvation. This promise of God is what leads to the setting of goals and the creating of a mission statement on the part of Christian organizations. The leading of the Holy Spirit and the practice of prayer direct us to the vision by which this promise becomes a specific goal and mission. The managing of Christian organizations is not merely the technique of setting goals, although it is that, too. But it is more than that. Effective management involves the discernment of the right goals, through prayer and the leading of the Holy Spirit. Goal setting indeed is a spiritual competence that the leadership of Christian organizations needs to develop.

Second, we understand God's providence as the outworking of his sovereign freedom and will, moving us toward promise through the history of those who seek to fulfill the promise. This is done through the church and its organizations. Christian organizations, as part of the church's apostolic mission in the world, embody the promise through their mission statements and goals. They "make history" through discerning the signs of the promise in the present, and through action plans that move into the future where God's providence will be revealed. Prayer and the leading of the Holy Spirit serve to liberate the plans and decisions of those who manage Christian organizations from a fatal identification of the sovereign will of God with any specific plan. Thus prayer and the

4. Ibid., pp. 190, 184.

leading of the Holy Spirit are continuing attendants to the process by which an organization projects goals through action plans. The "feedback" loop in the planning process not only includes adjustments due to evaluation of the actions taken in light of the goals, but of the goals themselves as evaluated through prayer and the illumination and direction of the Holy Spirit.

Third, we can now see that the spiritual life of the Christian organization is directed toward the practical wisdom by which an organization moves most effectively and efficiently toward its goals. A Christian organization may need to "winter in Fair Havens," based on the principle of common sense, but also to "launch out into the deep," based on the promise of Jesus.

Is it more "spiritual" to follow spiritual instincts than to give heed to common sense and follow spiritual expediency? Not at all. This kind of thinking is due more to religious mysticism than to the practical realism of incarnational Christianity. The Word of God was enfleshed and became a full participant in the business of living and working in this world. Thus, it is spiritual naiveté, not spiritual sense, in my judgment, that causes one to say, "My business is God's business, therefore all decisions are made by the Holy Spirit."

Those who think that prayer is a means by which decisions can be made "fail-safe" need to consider that Judas was an answer to prayer! After spending the night in prayer, Jesus called his disciples together, and out of a hundred possibilities chose twelve as the most likely to follow him in his mission and ministry (Luke 6:12-16). One of those twelve was Judas, who was eventually to betray him.

What are we to make of this? Jesus believed that the twelve were "those whom thou gavest me out of the world" (John 17:6). Does this mean that Jesus failed to discern the will of the Father in the case of Judas? Or does it mean that Judas was the "fateful" providence of God in the life of Jesus? In my judgment it was neither. What it does mean is that the choosing of the twelve was part of the "event" by which Jesus sought to carry out his messianic mission and purpose in obedience to the Father. Not all incidents that became part of this overall "event" were favorable, nor were all unhappy experiences. It was precisely because Jesus had prayed that he could give Judas the same chance that he gave to Peter, could "love them to the end," and could even wash their feet at the Last Supper (John 13).

It was through the prayer at the beginning that Jesus could accept even the tragic failure of Judas at the end as part of the overall purpose of God. The purpose and promise of God the Father as seen and sought by God the Son could not be thwarted or ultimately frustrated by decisions and plans that did not all work out perfectly.

In the end, you see, we are accountable—not to the plan but to the promise. We are accountable—not to be spiritual but to follow the lead of the Spirit of God, who seeks to glorify God through Christ. Thus, we are accountable, ultimately, not to the success of our own private projects nor to our own organizational goals but to the promise and goal as held forth by the kingdom of God as the consummation of Christ's ministry through the church. We are accountable not only to mind God's business but to manage it well, and to provide it with leadership that is capable of translating promise into plans and of infusing planning with hope.

In the end, minding God's business is a matter of effective leadership. Where is the leadership that is as concerned for the character of Christian organizations as for their purpose? Where is the leadership that issues out of a passion to be as true a servant of the organization as Jesus was of his own disciples, including Judas? What is the source of so much poor performance and ineffective management of Christian organizations?

Robert Greenleaf says it well:

> Who is the enemy? Who is holding back more rapid movement to the better society that is reasonable and possible with available resources? Who is responsible for the mediocre performance of so many of our institutions? Who is standing in the way of a larger consensus on the definition of the better society and paths to reach it? Not evil people. Not stupid people. Not apathetic people. Not the "system." . . . The real enemy is fuzzy thinking on the part of good, intelligent, vital people, and their failure to lead, and to follow servants as leaders.[5]

5. R. Greenleaf, *Servant Leadership* (New York: Paulist Press, 1977), pp. 44-45.

"God is the manager of this organization," said my friend. Don't you believe it! Yes, it is *God's* business, but *we* are the managers. And "blessed art thou if thou knowest what thou art doing!"

"You should have seen this land when God had it by himself," said the farmer to the preacher. I quite agree. God makes good sunsets, but we can do a better job of raising wheat. The question is, why are we not more effective in transforming the wheat into bread and feeding hungry and starving people? That's God's business too, and we are his managers.

God made reconciliation through Jesus Christ for all human persons, that they need not die but live eternally with him and share in the blessings of the kingdom of God forever. God did well in dying on a cross, but we are those commissioned to proclaim that event as the message of the gospel. The question is, why are we not more effective as agents of reconciliation, making disciples of "all the world"? That's God's business too, and we are his servant leaders.

Christian organizations, as an extension of the apostolic ministry of the church, are the means by which God's work continues to be done. Where there are none, and where God's work remains to be done, we should not hesitate to create new organizations. Where they already exist, we should renew and reinvigorate them with the wisdom and power of God through better leadership and management. This is what it is to mind God's business.

FOR FURTHER READING

The bibliographic resources listed here include representative selections from a rapidly expanding literature produced from both Christian and non-Christian perspectives. The titles are listed with brief annotations in most cases, but with no attempt to classify the listings into the several aspects of organizational management. Many of the titles listed here have been drawn from Edward R. Dayton, *Resources For Christian Leaders*, 7th ed. Monrovia, Calif.: MARC, n.d.

Adams, Arthur M. *Effective Leadership for Today's Church.* Philadelphia: Westminster Press, 1978. An excellent general resource on church politics. Discusses such issues as involving others in ministry, authority, and effectively running meetings.

Alexander, John W. *Managing Our Work.* Rev. ed. Downers Grove, Ill.: InterVarsity Press, 1975. Applies clearly articulated biblical principles to management, planning, execution, and review.

Allen, Daniel J., and Daniel L. Mead. *Ministry by Objectives.* Wheaton, Ill.: Evangelical Teacher Training Association, 1978. An approach to setting ministry goals that emphasizes objectives and strategies.

Allen, Louis A. *Making Managerial Planning More Effective.* New York: McGraw-Hill, 1982.

———. *The Management Profession.* New York: McGraw-Hill, 1964. Divides management work into four functions and establishes nineteen areas of management activity. Also provides applicable principles of management under related activities.

Anderson, James D., and Ezra E. Jones. *The Management of Ministry.* New York: Harper and Row, 1978. Focuses on parish ministry, and relates popular management theory to church life in the areas of leadership, purpose, structure, and community.

Anthony, Robert N., and David Young. *Management Control in Non-*

profit Organizations. 3d ed. Homewood, Ill.: Richard D. Irwin, 1983.

Argyris, Chris. *Integrating the Individual and the Organization.* New York: John Wiley and Sons, 1964. Discusses at length the continuous management problem of resolving individual goals with the requirements of corporate objectives.

Armerding, Hudson T. *Leadership.* Wheaton, Ill.: Tyndale House, l978. Excellent for inspiring a vision for leadership, especially the chapters on faith, handling succcess, and consistent growth.

Basil, Douglas C. "Leadership Skills and the Crisis of Change." *Humanitas* 14 (1978): 309-20. The author examines the dimensions of change effected by technology and suggests a new paradigm of leadership skills, including dealing with ambiguity, conflict, and complexity.

Bennis, Warren G. *Organization Development: Its Nature, Origins and Prospects.* Reading, Mass.: Addison-Wesley, 1969. A good introduction to emerging theories of organizational development.

Blanchard, Kenneth, and Spencer Johnson. *The One Minute Manager.* New York: Morrow, 1982. Already a classic, it provides helpful insights for motivating people in organizations.

Borst, Diane G., and Patrick J. Montana, eds. *Managing Non-Profit Organizations.* New York: American Management Association, l979. A compilation of articles, including "MBO in Church Organizations" and "The Future: Its Challenge and Promise."

Byron, William J., SJ. "The Purpose and Nature of Leadership." *New Catholic World* 223 (1980): 205-8. Sees the good leader as an enabler who empowers others and releases a potential in the follower. A biblical concept of leadership is found in service.

Campbell, Thomas C., and Gary B. Reierson. *The Gift of Administration: Theological Basis for Ministry.* Philadelphia: Westminster Press, 1981.

Campolo, Anthony. *The Success Fantasy.* Wheaton, Ill.: Victor Books, l980. Helpful in considering our visions in light of the success orientation of Western culture.

Churchman, C. West. *The Systems Approach.* Rev. and updated ed. New York: Dell, 1983. A useful introduction to the entire idea of systems and how they affect organizational structures. The author suggests that all systems must eventually end up with the consideration of value.

Cunningham, Agnes. "Pastoral Leadership in the Early Church."

Chicago Studies 17 (1978): 357-70. The focus is on pastoral leadership in the patristic era, with implications drawn out for pastoral leadership today.

Cyert, Richard M., and Lewis Benton. *The Management of Nonprofit Organizations.* Lexington, Mass.: Lexington Books, 1975.

Dayton, Edward R. *God's Purpose/Man's Plans.* Monrovia, Calif.: MARC, 1976. A workbook aimed at the manager involved in Christian organizations. Two programmed instructions aim at motivating people toward goal setting, one section is on planning, and one is on problem solving.

———. *Tools for Time Management.* Rev. ed. Grand Rapids: Zondervan, 1983. A "toolbox" of both techniques and principles for more effective time management.

Dayton, Edward R., and Ted W. Engstrom. *Strategy for Leadership.* Old Tappan, N.J.: Revell, 1979. Deals with a specific strategy for moving an organization ahead by focusing on the organization's purposes and goals and involving as many people as possible.

———. *Strategy for Living.* Glendale, Calif.: Regal, 1976. The authors' thesis is that one can apply the framework of goals, priorities, and planning to all of life.

Deegan, James, Jr. *The Priest as Manager.* New York: Bruce Publishing Co., 1969.

Dittes, James E. *When the People Say No.* San Francisco: Harper and Row, 1979. Helpful in providing insights into how to respond to opposition, conflict, and frustration.

Doohan, Helen. *Leadership in Paul.* Wilmington, Del.: Michael Glazier, 1984. Focusing on the nature of religious leadership from a Roman Catholic perspective, but applicable to the broad range of Christian leadership, this important book is based on a careful and scholarly analysis of Paul's leadership in the early church. Doohan suggests that Paul combined Spirit-directed vision and deep Christian conviction with a keen analysis of the present situation. The book includes an annotated bibliography of helpful resources in the area of religious leadership.

Drucker, Peter F. *Innovation and Entrepreneurship: Practice and Principles.* New York: Harper and Row, 1985. An examination of innovation and entrepreneurship as responsibilities of the executive's job that can and must be organized as systematic work.

———. *Management: Tasks, Practices, Responsibilities.* New York:

Harper and Row, 1974. This might be called Drucker's "magnum opus," in which he expounds his basic thinking on management and leadership.

———. *Managing in Turbulent Times.* New York: Harper and Row, 1980. Drucker's broad grasp of management economics, sociology, and history combine to paint a picture of tomorrow's organizations as well as of changes that will have to come about in management styles.

Dubin, Robert. *Human Relations in Administration.* 4th ed. Englewood Cliffs, N.J.: Prentice-Hall, 1974. A book of readings on the subject of human relations in organizations, drawn from a wide range of backgrounds and perspectives.

Ellis, Albert. *Executive Leadership: A Rational Approach.* New York: Institute for Rational Living, 1978. An approach to leadership based on application of the concepts of Rational Emotive Therapy.

Engel, James. *How Can I Get them to Listen?* Grand Rapids: Zondervan, 1977. A handbook for communication strategy, which is applicable to local church leadership.

Engstrom, Ted W. *The Making of a Christian Leader.* Grand Rapids: Zondervan, 1976. Covers the whole spectrum of leadership from the biblical basis to roles and activities of the Christian leader.

———. *Your Gift of Administration.* Nashville: Thomas Nelson, 1983. More helpful insights on applying sound principles of leadership skills from an accumulated reservoir of experience and biblical insight.

Engstrom, Ted W., and Edward R. Dayton. *The Art of Management for Christian Leaders.* Waco, Tex.: Word Books, 1976. A tightly packed management handbook that permits the reader to dip in at his or her point of interest.

———. *The Christian Executive.* Waco, Tex.: Word Books, 1979. Deals with the goals and relationships of the excutive. The book is divided into four parts: You and Yourself; You and Others; You and the Organization; and The Language of Management.

Ewing, David W. *The Human Side of Planning.* New York: Macmillan, 1969. One of the few books on planning that deal with all of the obstacles to making good planning work. It lays out in honest detail the type of human interaction that is needed to implement any plan.

Friesen, Garry, and J. Robin Maxson. *Decision Making and the Will of*

God. Portland, Oreg.: Multnomah Press, 1981. This book argues from a scriptural base, using many illustrations, to offer a realistic and valuable perspective on the relation of God's will to the process of decision making.

Galbraith, John K. *The Anatomy of Power*. Boston: Houghton Mifflin, l983. A keen analysis of the nature and use of power. Leaders of Christian organizations will gain crucial insights from this book.

Gangel, Kenneth O. *Competent to Lead*. Chicago: Moody Press, 1974. A serious attempt to integrate biblical theology and management.

————. *So You Want to Be a Leader*. Harrisburg, Pa.: Christian Publications, 1973. An excellent book on leadership from a Christian perspective.

Greenleaf, Robert. *The Servant as Religious Leader*. Windy Row Press, l982. A sequel to his classic book, *Servant Leadership*. New York: Paulist Press, 1977. Valuable insights into the role of leadership as applicable to Christian organizations.

Harris, Philip R., and Robert T. Moran. *Managing Cultural Differences*. Houston, Tex.: Gulf Publishing Co., 1979. This is vol. 1 of a two-volume series that is complemented by videotapes. The book deals with the emerging role of the multinational manager, the cultural impact of international management, and cultural specifics for management effectiveness. Includes a good number of case studies.

Harvanek, Robert. "The Expectations of Leadership." *Way* 15 (1975): 20-33. This excellent article begins by reflecting on the ambiguity of the contemporary need for leadership, not a leader. The author examines the community dimensions of leadership, with a different type of leadership demanded for each of several stages of community life.

Hemormesh, Richard, ed. *Strategic Management*. New York: John Wiley and Sons, 1983.

Hendrix, Olan. *Management for the Christian Worker*. Orange, Calif.: Quill Publications, 1976. This is an introduction to management as a type of work needed in all Christian organizations.

Henning, Margaret, and Ann Jardim. *The Managerial Woman*. Garden City, N.Y.: Anchor Press/Doubleday, 1981. Based on research conducted by the authors, the book sets out perceived differences in beliefs and assumptions that men and women hold about themselves, and how these differences affect management style.

Hersey, Paul. *The Situational Leader.* New York: Warner Books, 1984. A popularized readable digest of the situational leadership model developed by Hersey and Blanchard. A useful tool if not applied as a formula.

Hersey, Paul, and Kenneth A. Blanchard. *Management of Organizational Behavior: Utilizing Human Resources.* 4th ed. Englewood Cliffs, N.J.: Prentice-Hall, 1982.

Hodgkinson, Christopher. *The Philosophy of Leadership.* New York: St. Martin's Press, 1983. A look at leadership from a philosophical point of view. The leader is seen as philosopher in the organization, bringing values into the organizational realities.

Hughes, Charles L. *Goal Setting: Key to Organizational Effectiveness.* New York: American Management Association, 1965. Describes how overall objectives can be broken down into sub-goals for managers and employees at all levels.

Hutcheson, Richard G., Jr. *Wheel Within the Wheel.* Atlanta: John Knox, 1979. Confronts the management crisis of the pluralistic church. A fine resource for understanding the leader's role in managing, coordinating, and negotiating.

Kotler, Philip. *Marketing for Nonprofit Organizations.* 2d ed. Englewood Cliffs, N.J.: Prentice-Hall, 1982. Deals with techniques and concepts in marketing to analyze the needs of consumers, clients, supporters, and other publics with the idea of improving services and communications.

Kreider, Carl. *The Christian Entrepreneur.* Scottdale, Pa.: Herald Press, 1980. Deals with the productive use of wealth, Christian ethics in business, concepts of a Christian standard of living, and creative Christian alternative forms of business. Ends with a chapter on the unique gifts of the entrepreneur to the church.

Leas, Speed B. *Leadership and Conflict.* Nashville: Abingdon, 1982. A systematic approach to handling the politics and conflicts of leadership in a voluntary organization.

Lewis, Douglass. *Resolving Church Conflicts.* San Francisco: Harper and Row, 1981. A case study approach to help the reader understand how conflicts emerge and how to resolve them with positive results.

Lippitt, Gordon L. *Organizational Renewal: A Holistic Approach to Organization Development.* 2d ed. Englewood Cliffs, N.J.: Prentice-Hall, 1982.

MacDonald, Gordon. *Ordering Your Private World.* Chicago: Moody

Press, 1984. Integrates spiritual direction and vision with the pragmatic details of personal management.

McGregor, Douglas. *The Human Side of Enterprise*. New York: McGraw-Hill, 1960. Compares two theories of human behavior: theory X assumes that the average worker doesn't like to work and does so under duress; theory Y assumes that work is natural to human persons and that motivation is dependent upon how well human needs can be satisfied. A management classic.

Mackenzie, Alec, and Kay C. Waldo. *About Time! A Woman's Guide to Time Management*. New York: McGraw-Hill, 1981. Views many of the typical time management tools from a woman's perspective.

McSwain, Larry, and William D. Treadwell, Jr. *Conflict Ministry in the Church*. Nashville: Broadman, 1981. Strategies for resolving conflict and stress.

Mager, Robert F. *Goal Analysis*. 2d ed. Belmont, Calif.: Pitman Learning, 1984. A helpful book with some programmed instructions that will help people understand the difference between real goals and fuzzy goals.

Moltmann, Jürgen. *Hope and Planning*. New York: Harper and Row, 1971. In this book, Moltmann applies his "Theology of Hope" to the process of planning. Helpful for those who have some theological training.

O'Toole, James. *The Corporate Vanguard: An Agenda for the New Management*. New York: Doubleday, 1985. Focuses on excellence as a limitation of greatness.

Padovano, Anthony T. "Leadership and Authority." *New Catholic World* 223 (1980): 222-24. Considers the nature of authority and the character of leadership in terms of the church.

Perry, Lloyd, and Norman Shawchuck. *Revitalizing the Twentieth-Century Church*. Chicago: Moody Press, 1982. A practical guide to renewal with emphasis on planning to make visions come true.

Peters, Thomas J., and Nancy Austin. *A Passion for Excellence: The Leadership Difference*. New York: Random House. The sequel to *In Search of Excellence* (see below), it boils the original eight principles of excellence down to four and the role of leadership in implementation.

Peters, Thomas J., and Robert H. Waterman, Jr. *In Search of Excellence*. New York: Harper and Row, 1982. Identifies the qualities that distinguish the top corporations in the United States.

Reddin, W. J. *Effective Management by Objectives: The 3-D Method of MBO*. New York: McGraw-Hill, 1971. A readable discussion of MBO (management by objectives), pointing out its basic principles as well as its dangers.

Richards, Lawrence, and Clyde Hoeldtke. *A Theology of Church Leadership*. Grand Rapids: Zondervan, 1980. Examines the relationship between secular management tools and leadership within the local church. While rejecting the use of secular management concepts for the local church, the authors find many of these understandings useful in managing the "enterprises" of the local church.

Rush, Myron. *Management: A Biblical Approach*. Wheaton, Ill.: Victor Books, 1983.

Sanders, Oswald J. *Spiritual Leadership*. Rev. ed. Chicago: Moody Press, 1980. Deals with the spiritual dimension of the leader's life.

Schaller, Lyle E. *The Change Agent*. Nashville: Abingdon, 1972. Recommended for those who wish to understand more about the dynamics of being a "change agent" in Christian organizations.

_____. *The Decision-Makers: How to Improve the Quality of Decision-Making in the Churches*. Nashville: Abingdon, 1974.

_____. *Effective Church Planning*. Nashville: Abingdon, 1979. An excellent integration of Schaller's concepts, including his understanding of the difference between small groups and large groups, with several planning models described. It is more a theory of planning than a "how to" book.

_____. *Parish Planning*. Nashville: Abingdon, 1971. An excellent idea- as well as sourcebook on "how to get things done in the church."

Schaller, Lyle E., and Charles A. Tidwell. *Creative Church Adminstration*. Nashville: Abingdon, 1975. Looks at planning by beginning with value analysis, moves to planning models, discusses motivation, and then deals with enlisting and developing volunteer leaders.

Schein, Edgar H. *Organizational Culture and Leadership: A Dynamic View*. San Francisco: Jossey-Bass, 1985. A scholarly publication out of MIT that focuses on the role of leadership in developing the culture of the organization.

Sine, Tom. *The Mustard Seed Conspiracy*. Waco, Tex.: Word Books, 1981. A futurologist's view of what the church must do in order to respond to the trends for the future.

Snyder, Howard A. *Liberating the Church.* Downers Grove, Ill.: Inter-
Varsity Press, 1982. Emphasizes the kingdom of God as the
church's primary goal.
Steiner, George A. *Strategic Planning: What Every Manager Must Know.*
New York: Free Press, 1979.
Vroom, Victor H., and Edward L. Deci, eds. *Management and Moti-
vation.* New York: Penguin Books, 1971.
Werning, Waldo J. *Vision and Strategy for Church Growth.* 2d ed. Grand
Rapids: Baker Book House, 1983. The need for faith and vision
is balanced with proper planning.
Wilson, Marlene. *The Effective Management of Volunteer Programs.*
Boulder, Colo.: Volunteer Management Associates, 1976. A
compact synthesis of a great deal of management research pack-
aged in a way to be understandable to the beginning manager,
and for those who manage volunteer organizations.
Wright, J. "Led by the Spirit." *Way* 15 (1975): 11-19. The author
suggests that the perspective on leadership in the Christian community is that of leadership as the gift and work of the Spirit.
Providing a scriptural basis for this perspective, he develops two
dimensions of leadership as a focus on goals and community.
Yukl, Gary. *Leadership in Organizations.* Englewood Cliffs, N.J.: Prentice-Hall, 1981.

INDEX